D1046293

WINGS OF PRAYER

SISTER ÍDE M. NÍ RIAIN, RCSJ
AND
BROTHER KENNETH, CGA

WINGS OF PRAYER
MEDITATING ON SCRIPTURE

HarperCollins*Religious*
An Imprint of HarperCollins*Publishers*

HarperCollins*Religious*
Part of HarperCollins*Publishers*
77–85 Fulham Palace Road,
Hammersmith, London W6 8JB

First published in Great Britain
in 1992 by HarperCollins*Religious*

Copyright © 1992 Sister Íde M. Ní Riain, RSCJ
and Brother Kenneth, Community of the Glorious Ascension

The Authors assert the moral right to be
identified as the authors of this work

A catalogue record for this book
is available from the British Library

ISBN 0 00 599251 6

Printed in Great Britain by
HarperCollinsManufacturing Glasgow

Conditions of Sale
This book is sold subject to the condition that it
shall not, by way of trade or otherwise, be lent, re-sold,
hired out or otherwise circulated without the publisher's
prior consent in any form of binding or cover other
than that in which it is published and without a
similar condition including this condition being
imposed on the subsequent purchaser.

To Mary
Mother of God

ACKNOWLEDGEMENTS

This anthology owes its genesis to Dom Placid Murray, OSB of Glenstal Abbey, Eire who persuaded Sister Íde, many years ago, to translate that great *chef d'oeuvre* of St Ambrose: *In Psalmum CXVIII Expositio*. Sister Íde's deep gratitude is also due to her Brother, Dom Vincent Ryan, OSB librarian at Glenstal, and Father Fleury, SJ librarian at Milltown Park who made accessible the Latin text from which the translation was made. Both Sister Íde and Brother Kenneth, whose role has been to edit and on occasion rewrite, rather than to translate, wish to thank their respective communities at Mount Anville in Dublin and Telford in Shropshire for their invariable patience and understanding.

CONTENTS

CONTENTS

CONTENTS

INTRODUCTION: CHRISTIAN MEDITATION

The Psalms of the Old Testament, chanted or recited as they are by the Church all over the world, day after day, are a particularly suitable basis for Christian meditation. They are a cry from the depths of the human heart. Viewed as prophecy, they foretell the life of Christ. Viewed mystically, they are the prayer of Christ, which he prays in each one of us.

Psalm 118 (119) is a compendium or microcosm of the whole of Scripture. It is a poem, of one hundred and seventy-six verses, in praise of the divine Law or divine righteousness. God's decrees, statutes and judgements are viewed by the Psalmist as a light for one's path and a lantern for one's way (cf. v. 105). The psalm abounds in metaphors. In it one can see the Passion of our Lord foretold: his persecution, "The snares of the wicked encompassed me" (v. 61); his trial, "Though Princes sit and plot together against me" (v. 23); "The proud have smeared him with lies" (v. 69); His judgement, "I have been afflicted beyond measure" (v. 107); His vindication by the Father, "They have almost made an end of me on the earth: But I have not forsaken your precepts. In your merciful goodness give me life" (vv. 87–8).

We hear the cry of the poor, the complaint of the oppressed, "Turn aside the taunts that I dread" (v. 39); "Trouble and anguish have taken hold on me" (v. 143); the secret prayer of the saint, "If only my ways were unerring" (v. 5); "I am but a stranger on the earth" (v. 19); "Order my steps according to your word: that no evil may get mastery over me" (v. 133). All of these elements are joined together by an overriding theme: the sheer beauty of God's Law.

Our guide in Christian meditation on this Psalm is St Ambrose (see Appendix). This great Father of the Church was familiar with every page of Scripture, but especially loved the Psalms, and wrote innumerable commentaries on them. The Bible used by Christians in the fourth century differed in some places from the versions we use today, but we can be quite sure that the Holy Spirit was as much in charge then as he is now. Meditation as practised and taught by Ambrose is very much a matter of letting the Holy Spirit be your guide. You take the Psalm verse by verse, reflecting on it until a variety of meanings begins to unfold, talking to our Lord about it, and forming inner resolutions for the day.

Each verse connects with other passages from Scripture: the whole Bible, in fact, has an inner unity due to the inspiration of the Holy Spirit, despite the variety of human authors and editors. Ambrose particularly liked connecting the Psalms with the Song of Songs.

Those of you who have never prayed using the Bible in this way might find the following helpful. Begin by reading the Scripture verse at the head of the page you have chosen; for example, "The earth, O Lord, is full of your loving mercy" (v. 64). Commit it to your memory and repeat it to yourself over and over again in the course of the day. In this way it will come to life and you will begin to "see" it. At the time you have selected for your meditation seat yourself so that you are comfortable but also alert, perhaps beginning with the sign of the Cross or some other physical prayer, and then go through the appropriate printed section slowly and thoughtfully. The words will begin to come to life, and thoughts, lights and ideas of your own will start to surface. Meanings will dawn on you, and, to use a comparison from Ambrose himself, "Suddenly, as though appearing over the hills, the Word will illumine our mind and make clear what previously had seemed incomprehensible." Every so often there is a wonderful moment when Christ seems to come to life in the text, and one senses that there is actually someone looking over one's shoulder. A good way to end might be to use the Scripture verse with which you began in prayer to God to redirect your heart towards him. In this way the meditation will be acting as a leaven in your day:

"The Earth, O Lord, is full of your loving mercy: teach me your statutes."

1

THE BODY OF CHRIST:
SECRET CHAMBER OF
THE CHURCH

I will praise you, O Lord, with an upright heart;
when I shall have learned the righteousness of
your justice. (Psalm 119:7, 8)

Meditation

The Psalmist is anxious to learn the deep secrets of
God, to enter the inmost mysteries of heaven. The
bride in the poet-king's Song of Songs cries, "Draw us
after you, we shall run in the sweetness of your
fragrance. The King has brought me into his secret
room" (Song 1:3).

Reflection

Whose are these mysteries: where is this secret room?
The mysteries are those of the King of Heaven. The
secret room is his Passion. There he shows to his bride,
who is the Church, his blood flowing from his pierced
side and his body being anointed for burial. And she
sees the mystery of his Resurrection. But once led into
Christ's secret chamber, the Church is not merely
betrothed; she is already married. She enters the bridal

room and is given the keys of lawful consummation. "Let him kiss me with his own lips" (Song 1:1). Thus is the gracious outpouring of the Holy Spirit described. His descent, so to speak, is a kiss. As the Angel says to Mary, "The Holy Spirit will come upon you and the power of the most High will overshadow you." Happy in the bridal chamber the Church, or the individual Christian soul, says, "My brother is sweet myrrh to me, he lies upon my breast" (Song 1:12).

Prayer

Lord, you teach me that I must enter my innermost being, my secret place and with the door closed pray to our Father in secret. The Church, Christ's Body, is the secret chamber. There you, our King, lead us into the deepest mysteries. You have given your Church the keys with which she can unlock for herself the treasures of the sacraments and the doors of knowledge. There we can discover how to rest in you; the grace of the sleep of death and the power of your resurrection. You have brought me into your secret room. I will praise you, O Lord, with an upright heart.

2

THE CALL OF JOHN

How shall a young man's path be pure; unless he keep to your word? (Psalm 119:9)

Meditation

In John the apostle you have a young man who remained pure. He was a fisherman with his father and brother. One day as they were mending their nets, John saw the Lord Jesus, and heard him saying, "Follow me, and I will make you fishers of men" (Matthew 4:19). With his brother James, John left his nets and their father, and followed Jesus. John had begun to earn his living as a fisherman, but once he had heard Christ's command he proved that a young man can remain pure by behaving as God's word prescribes. He opened his eyes, saw the straight way and left the crooked one. He said, "The upright love you" (Song 1:3), but the twisted and the crooked do not. Only the path of righteousness and justice has power to reach you. One who loves justice does not turn away from Christ, and an innocent conscience is not afraid of the judge who judges justly and rewards the good.

Reflection

In John we see a wonderful mystery as expressed by the Royal Bridegroom when inspired to compose the Song of Songs. I can picture the Lord Jesus at the banquet, and John leaning his head on Jesus' breast. All the others are amazed that sinful flesh should repose upon the temple of the Word, that a soul bound by the bonds of sinful flesh should search the divine depths of that heavenly hall. But John replies in the words of the Song of Songs, "I am dark but beautiful, daughters of Jerusalem" (Song 1:5). Dark through sin, beautiful through grace. And our flesh says, "I am dark but beautiful." Dark with the dust of this world, beautiful with the oil of the Spirit.

Prayer

I am dark through my wickedness, but beautiful now through baptism. I am dark because I have sinned, but beautiful because you love me. I was repudiated and rejected in my mother Eve; but you receive me and welcome me back in my mother Mary. Let me keep to your Word and then my path shall be pure.

3

THE BALSAM TREE

Grant this to me, your servant; let me live, and living, keep your word. (Psalm 119:17)

Meditation

Christ likes to be served. Happy are those who serve Him. She who replied to Gabriel, "I am the Lord's servant; as you have spoken, so be it", glowed brightly with the balm of grace – and conceived. Thus the Lord Jesus clothed Himself with the sacred sign of his humanity. "My brother," she cries "is a bundle of myrrh between my breasts" (Song 1:12). By taking our flesh, the Lord Jesus bound himself with the cords of love. He fastened himself not only to our limbs and natural passions, but even to the cross. The poet-king speaks of the vines of Engedi: "My brother is fragrant spikenard among the vines of Engedi" (Song 1:13). Engedi is believed to be a place in Judaea where the balsam tree grows; a tree which, if gashed, yields a fragrant balm. If you do not cut the tree, the balm will refuse to flow. Once its bark has been cut by the hand of a master, the tears begin to fall; just as the tears of Christ, crucified on the Tree, were shed to wash away the sins of the people, a balm poured from a merciful heart. On that Tree he cried, "Father, forgive them; they do not know what they are doing" (Luke 23:34).

Reflection

If I understand you aright, when the balsam tree is pierced, balm squeezes out through the cut that the woodman has made. So Jesus, when he is pierced, pours out the balm that is the remission of our sins and our redemption? When the Word became flesh, he was bound. He who possesses all things became poor to enrich us by his poverty. The Almighty made himself contemptible, so that Herod despised and mocked him. He who moves the earth was nailed fast to a tree. He who veils the heavens in deep darkness was crucified; he bowed his head in death, yet his word went out into all the world.

Prayer

Lord, you surrendered your life and you fill all things. You came down to earth and we are taken up to heaven. You were made flesh so that humanity might claim the place of the Word at the right hand of the Father. A wound has been inflicted and healing ointment has flowed out. The worm cried out, and you, God, were recognised. Grant this to me, your servant; let me live, and living, keep your word.

4

SHADOW LAND

Grant this to me your servant: let me live, and living keep your word. (Psalm 119:17)

Meditation

In this life we are not really living. On earth it is but a shadow, an image of life, not the reality. It is as if mankind were walking in a reflection, for we dwell in the valley of the shadow of death. If, however, we were to raise our eyes from earthly to spiritual things, and if we were to say, "The breath of our nostrils is Christ the Lord," we should be worthy to add, "Under your shadow we shall live" (Lamentations 4:20). David, the Lord's chosen one, declares, "In the shadow of your wings hide me" (Psalm 16:8). Even the Saints are in the shadow so long as they are in this body. They do not see perfectly. They know only in part. As Paul says, "our knowledge is imperfect" (1 Corinthians 13:9). Yet Paul was the chosen instrument whose eyes Christ opened after that blinding light. Paul did not see face to face but only a reflection as in a glass.

Reflection

We live in the shadow, and in his shadow we keep the words of God. When people were under the shadow of the Law, they kept the Sabbath, which is a shadow of the future. We, too, who live by the Gospel, follow the shadow of the Word of God. Nathaniel, we read, was in the shade of a fig tree; the Psalmist sings of his hopes in the shadow of the wings of the Lord Jesus; Zachaeus climbed into the shade of a sycamore tree to see Christ. Jesus stretches out his hands to us, too, that he may overshadow the whole world. How can we fail to be in his shadow, we who are protected by the veil of his cross?

Prayer

I know that you did not come into this world with the glory which was yours from the beginning. You emptied yourself and came in the form of a servant. In the power of the Holy Spirit, overshadowing Mary, you came so that you might transfigure this lowly body of ours and make it like your own in glory. Grant this to me, your servant: let me live, and living keep your Word.

5

THE EYES OF THE SOUL

Take away the veil from my eyes: that I may see the wonders of your law. (Psalm 119:18)

Meditation

Those who ask to have their eyes opened know that their eyelids are held fast . . . So the patient says to the doctor that comes from heaven, "Take away the veil from my eyes". There is a certain condition, an affliction that impairs our sight. As in such a case we need a good doctor to remove the veil, the cataracts that cover our eyes preventing us from seeing what we used to see, so, too, there is a way we may remove the cataract from the eyes of the heart. Be turned to the Lord and the veil will fall away. Paul was converted when, after Ananias blessed him, the scales fell from his eyes. After not having seen for three days, he began to see. At one and the same moment for Paul, his bodily eyes and the eyes of his soul were healed; the Doctor from heaven had shown the remedy. It is written of him that, he sent his word and healed them: and "he set them free from their infirmities" (Psalm 107:20 LXX).

Reflection

Not of this earth is the physician who cures all infirmities and heals entire nations. Even the apostles' eyes were closed until Jesus opened them. Those two walking sadly home to their village Emmaus, after his crucifixion. He opened their eyes as he interpreted the scriptures. And when he blessed the bread at supper, their "eyes were opened and they recognised him" (Luke 24:31). On the mountain, Peter's eyes were closed, John's were closed and his brother's were closed as well. All three were heavy with sleep; but when the splendour of divine majesty roused them, they opened the eyes of their hearts.

Prayer

Unless Jesus first opens our eyes, not one of us will see him. Until he first removes the cataract, in none of us will the grace of the Gospel shine. Father, we ask you to send us this physician. Let your Word come; and please may he open my eyes. Take away the veil from my eyes; that I may see the wonders of your law.

6

SACRAMENTAL CONFESSION

Unveil my eyes and I will gaze upon the marvels of your law. (Psalm 119:18)

Meditation

Among the marvels of the new law, the law of love, is the great wonder of forgiveness. In the Gospel of St Luke we read of a leper coming to Jesus and saying to him, "If you want to, you can cure me" (5:12) Leprosy was not only a foul disease; it was also seen as a type of sin. Jesus's reply to the poor man, "Of course, I want to," is the straightforward loving response of our Saviour to human need and an assertion of his desire to heal our transgressions as well. The leper saw that the will of the Lord was all that was necessary for this power to be made available. Christ does not want us to sin. It is his will that everyone should be clean. He touched the leper. He touches all those who have faith. Again in St Luke he exclaims, "Who touched me? I felt that power had gone from me" (8:46). A Christian has in the Eucharist the grace of his pure Body and Blood, and forgiveness from God himself.

Reflection

The story of the cleansing of the leper ends with the Lord instructing the man, "opening his eyes" as the Psalmist puts it, to show himself to the priest (Luke 5:14). The synagogue had many priests, but he whose eyes are opened does not see the false priests, but only the true priest. Who else can that true priest be, but he who is priest for ever, as the Father says to him. "You are a priest for ever" (Psalm 109:4). The leper, with his eyes opened, saw and understood what kind of gift he must offer in thanksgiving for having been made clean.

Prayer

Lord, happy is the one who hears these things, but happier still are those who see and are able to show themselves to the Priest. They have nothing which they must fear to reveal to him. Unless we are prepared to see ourselves as we are, we remain like Adam who tried to hide himself. He had forgotten that he had been created by God. Unveil my eyes and I will gaze upon the marvels of your law.

7

THE GRACE OF
HUMILITY

Turn away from me their reproach and scorn: for
I have kept your commands. (Psalm 119:22)

Meditation

In the first letter of Paul to the church at Corinth we
read, "Those whom the world thinks common and
contemptible are the ones that God has chosen"
(1 Corinthians 1:28). But how then can the Psalmist ask
that reproach and scorn be averted? We have to
understand that Paul was speaking of what is contemptible not in God's sight, but in the eyes of the
world. That which is contemptible in this world is
precious in the sight of God: humility, for example. In
this world it is despised, but highly approved of in
God's judgement. The publican, when he humbles
himself, is the one who is commended. Would you like
to know who is loved by God, and who is considered
important by God? The person who is holy; who lives
a life without stain; who keeps his word; does not
wrong his neighbour; is not pining for other people's
possessions, and "in whose eyes the worthless have no
honour; but who makes much of those that fear the
Lord" (Psalm 15:4).

Reflection

We must however take care never to be cursed by Christ. I should not like anyone to curse and despise me as a sinner, but how terrible if Christ were to say of me as he said of Chorazin and Bethsaida, "Alas for you Chorazin; alas for you Bethsaida . . ." (Luke 10:13). They were condemned because they did not repent of their sins. We must behave in such a way as to get rid of sin, but can there be anyone who is without reproach? Yes, the lover of God's commandments.

Prayer

Lord there are plenty of people who like to insult your servants, but they must not be a discouragement. As for me, it is my glory to suffer insult for your name. Turn away from me their reproach and scorn; for I have kept your commands.

8

PRINCES OF DARKNESS

Princes sit and plot together against me; but your servant shall meditate on your statutes. (Psalm 119:23)

Meditation

In the Letter to the Ephesians we read about some of these princes. "It is not against human enemies that we have to struggle, but against sovereignties and the powers who originate the darkness in this world, the spiritual army of evil in the heavens" (Ephesians 6:12). These are they who confer together to see who in this world is just, who is a Christian, intent on serving God, who is zealous for every good cause. Once these are found, they lay their plots. "Let us lie in wait", they say; "let us set a trap. Let us prevent the plans for good from bring implemented. Let us break spirits and destroy souls by subtle and repeated blows. If God loves them, if they are so just, let us ask leave to test them by temptations."

Reflection

Surely they could never have had such power over a prophet like David unless the Lord allowed it? The Lord wanted to prove the worth of his soldier that he might crown him with glory. Who roused up the spirit of King Saul against David? Was it not the evil spirit who did not like being expelled whenever David played the harp? By the sweet harmony and his own skilful playing on the strings, David could soothe the mind and heart of the king. Who but Satan awoke the wickedness dormant in Doeg the Syrian, making him reveal the priest who had shown kindness and hospitality to David? Who inflamed the sinful lust of Ammon so that he committed incest in his own father's palace, saddening David's heart by the horror perpetrated by one child and the outrage suffered by another? Who armed the fury of Absalom, so that he turned his own father out of his house and then pursued him, bent on his death?

Prayer

Lord, when everything had gone against David, and his army was weak and outnumbered, by reason of that very weakness the powers that raged against him were defeated. And though the son sought his father's death, David in tender love commanded that the life of his son should be spared. You did not spare your Son but gave him up for us all to destroy the powers of evil. They plot together against me, but your servant shall meditate on your statutes.

9

SORROW AND
AMENDMENT

I have declared my ways and you have heard me;
teach me your statutes. (Psalm 119:26)

Meditation

In "declaring his ways" the Psalmist admits his faults
and is not silent before God. He confesses that he was
wrong, and does not conceal his lapses. In another
Psalm we read, "In the presence of the Lord I will
confess my faults" (31:5). When just women or just
men accuse themselves like this, they silence those who
were getting ready to accuse them – to add to their
guilt or exaggerate their sins. The just, anticipating the
attack, by confession seals an adversary's lips and so
prepares the way for pardon. True sorrow excuses
guilt. Genuine shame accuses Satan who is the author
of sin.

Reflection

When a person admits that he has sinned, he is
obviously sorry for what he has done – or rather for
what he was tricked into doing by the devil's cunning.
Is that why Scripture says, "The just man begins by
accusing himself" (Proverbs 18:17)? Whoever accuses

himself, even though he is a sinner, begins to be just. Unsparing towards himself, he confesses that God is just. Such a person does not believe that anything can be hidden from God.

Prayer

Lord, if only Adam had begun by accusing himself instead of hiding! Yet confession by itself is not enough. If I want to be corrected I must ask you to teach me your commandments, to avoid error in the future. Thus the Psalmist asks to be taught by you, for you are our master. It is not those taught by men who are blessed but those whom you instruct (cf. Psalm 93:12). I have declared my ways and you have heard me; teach me your statutes.

10

MEDITATION

Make me to understand the way of your precepts:
and I shall meditate on your marvellous works.
(Psalm 119:27)

Meditation

The Psalmist, like a good judge and discerner of truth
about himself, was prepared to be taught to the point of
weariness or until it felt as though he could understand
no more. He was prepared to spend many long hours,
over and above those he ought to have spent, even
going beyond the bounds of his own strength in order
to meditate on the marvellous works of God. It would
be a prolonged meditation almost as painful to the
mind as the exercises of the gymnast in the gymnasium.
In the story of Isaac, waiting anxiously for Rebecca,
(the bride whom his servant was bringing home for
him), we read that "Isaac went out into the fields to
meditate" (Genesis 24:63). That is how we read it in
the Septuagint. In the Latin bible the word is translated
"to take a stroll." Thus we read, "Isaac went out into
the fields to take a stroll."

Reflection

I understand. Rebecca was on her way. Rebecca, in whom we see the church prefigured. In the marriage that was being prepared is another sign. Isaac, aware of these great mysteries, goes out into the fields. He has shed every anxiety and walks in innocence of heart. He thinks deeply on various matters, and rejoices in all that God has done. The Psalmist, too, wants to imitate Isaac, to be taught God's statutes and to learn the path of heaven's commandments.

Prayer

Keep me awake to you. Do not let me be seduced by the glamour of empty things, nor diverted from the pursuit of truth. Make me to understand the way of your precepts: and I shall meditate on your marvellous works.

11

THE BEAUTY OF
SILENCE

My soul has melted away for weariness: strengthen
me in your words. (Psalm 119:28)

Meditation

In the Book of Proverbs we read, "My son, do not talk
too much" (3:21). One who is forever talking is like a
leaking roof, gushing first this way and then that;
always pouring out his entire self. "My soul has melted
away – leaked away." External things will swamp him,
for he has no place of shelter. He is quite unable to keep
anything to himself. Oh, that such a one would learn of
Blessed Mary who kept everything in her heart so that
she would lose nothing! The holy Church, however,
claims that she is worthy to entertain her husband
Christ. He is the guest whom she invites, but she will
not appear before him unless she is suitably dressed.
Faithfully preserving silence she says, "How beautiful
you are, my love, how beautiful you are! All green is
our bed. The beams of our house are of cedar, the
panelling of cypress" (Song 1:16–17).

Reflection

The Church rightly adores the beauty of the One whom she loves, and whom she praises more by silent love. The faithful interpreter of his mysteries preaches more by silence than by words, for he who divulges the secret mysteries diminishes Christ's beauty. Let no one cast pearls before swine, lest those precious jewels are trampled under foot. Christ will not lay his head in the house of one who is simply a great talker or gossip. For where there is too much talk, sin will find its way in.

Prayer

Holy Spirit, help me seriously to provide a place worthy of Christ. May I be careful in what I say, and not talk too much. May I be straightforward but not self-important. Strengthen me in your words.

12

THE HOUSE OF CEDAR

My soul has melted away for weariness: strengthen me in your words. (Psalm 119:28)

Meditation

If a Christian who does not know how to be still is like a house with a leaky roof, the Church by the same token is like a sound house, praising in silent love the Lord who is her husband. In the Song of Songs we read, "The beams of our house are of cedar", and it is well to remember that so great is the beauty of cedar that the sweet singer of Israel in the Psalms can think of no better way of describing the glory of the people of God than to compare them with that tree. "So the virtuous flourish like palm trees and grow as tall as the cedars of Lebanon" (91:13). Just as cedar wood does not decay, the glory of Israel is not corrupted by old age.

Reflection

We read in the same Song of Songs, "the panelling of our house is of cypress" (1:16). Cypress is a species that is always green. Winter, spring and summer, it keeps its luxuriant foliage, and never changes colour. Alone among trees it is never stripped by the wind of its glory. Alone it never sheds its old garments nor clothes itself anew. So, too, the grace of the Gospel never fails; though as old as the apostles it is evergreen.

Prayer

If we live in you and you live in us, we are like the cypress and will not experience corruption. Instead we shall hold up for ever patiently and in greatness of heart the pillars of justice and all other virtues. But, Lord, when my soul melts away for weariness: strengthen me in your words.

13

CHRIST THE
CHARIOTEER

Let me run the way of your commandments: for
you will liberate my heart. (Psalm 119:32)

Meditation

Saint Paul in the first letter to the Christians at Corinth
tells them they, "must run to win" (9:28). Whoever
runs like that will be able to declare, "I have run the
race to the finish" (2 Timothy 4:7). I have run like a
noble steed. Yes, Christ has his steeds. The prophet
spoke of them when he said, "You have trampled the
sea with your horses: and the mighty waters boil"
(Habakkuk 3:15). It is as though Habakkuk were
talking about the Apostles who, by preaching the
Gospel, have stirred up the pagan nations; nations that
were tossed up and down like mighty waters, restless as
the waves of the sea. Preaching the Good News has
turned the nations from their idols and led them to faith
in Christ. Earlier in the same chapter the prophet had
said, "You come mounted on your horses, on your
victorious chariots" (3:8). O wonderful team of twelve
horses; your harness is peace and your reins charity.
Bound to each other by the cords of love, they submit
to the yoke of faith, while the four wheels of their

chariot is the mystery of the Gospel which they carry to the ends of the earth.

Reflection

You are right, it is a noble chariot, and its charioteer is the Word of God. His whip puts to flight all wordly longings. He banishes the prince of this world so that the righteous can run their race to the finish. O splendid race of truly wise horses, a marvellous mystery! The wheels that run so smoothly beneath the chariot are the New Testament that is contained within the Old. Like the wheels, the New Covenant ran within the very vehicle by which it was contained. The wheels ran in four places and were never forced to retreat. The Spirit of life was in those who ran to the four corners of the earth; and they ran smoothly because the life of those horses was blameless, and he who rode them never slept.

Prayer

You, Jesus, are the charioteer of my soul. You want to rein in my body too. You remain for ever watchful over me for you are not like the horseman of the Psalmist who mounted and slept (75:7). The sea of sloth must be crossed, and with difficulty even by those who keep awake. Those who were to fall asleep would certainly never cross it. They would drown like those Egyptians who perished body and soul. As Scripture says, "Horses and rider he has thrown into the sea"

(Exodus 15:1). Instead of keeping the law they persecuted it. Let me run the way of your commandments: for you will liberate my heart.

14

CHRIST OUR GENERAL

Teach me, O Lord, the way of your statutes.
(Psalm 119:33)

Meditation

A soldier, when he sets out on a route march, does not
decide for himself what kit he is carrying, nor does he
please himelf in deciding which way or with whom he
is to go. He neither does what he wants, nor does he
desert the colours. He receives his orders from his
commanding officer, and he obeys them. He follows
the route marked out for him, he has his arms at the
ready and he completes his march as ordered so as to
reach the food and rest prepared for him. If he does go
off in another direction he will never get his rations,
nor find the resting place prepared for him. The general
sees that all these things are provided for those who
faithfully follow him, not turning aside either to right
or to left. If a soldier follows his own general he will
make no mistakes, for his commanding officer is not
concerned for his own interests, but sets a steady pace
so that all will be able to keep up.

Reflection

To continue your metaphor, the general will have picked out in advance the towns where his soldiers can rest, for three or four days or even longer. That will depend on the abundance there of water and supplies. Thus the soldiers continue their march without undue fatigue, until they reach the royal city where weary armies find their rest. I recognise God's law as the way marked out for us to march along. Christ is our commander-in-chief, our general, and the saints our fellow-marchers. Our ancestors, too, the old Israel, marched from the land of Egypt, covering great distances, taking refreshment at many points, at the resting places marked out for them along the route. God went before them, by day in the form of a pillar of cloud, to provide shade for the travellers; by night in the form of a pillar of fire, to show them the way and to give them light. When he wanted to give his army a rest from marching, the pillar of fire came to a halt, and the shining cloud did not move. When he wanted them to move on, forward went the pillar of fire by night and the pillar of cloud by day.

Prayer

Father, that pillar of cloud moving before the Israelites must have been beautiful. Mysteriously it signifies the coming of the Lord Jesus in a pure cloud, as Isaiah says. The cloud is the Mother of your Son, the Virgin Mary, because of her descent from Eve. She is pure because, though a mother, she remained a virgin. Pure too, because she sought not to please the world, but to please you. Pure because her womb became fruitful by the overshadowing of the Holy Spirit. She brought forth her child not in sin, but in grace. Teach me her obedience; instruct me, O Lord, in the way of your statutes.

15

CHRIST AND THE CHURCH

Teach me, O Lord, the way of your statutes: and I will honour it to the end. (Psalm 119:33)

Meditation

As she walks along the way of the Lord it can be said of the Church that she is, "the flower of the fields and the lily among the thorns" (Song 2:1–2). The faith of the Church has gone out into all the world and thus have Christ's footsteps been imprinted on its surface. It is right, therefore, to call her the flower of the fields. Surely that is what Saint Paul was saying when he wrote, "We are Christ's sweet fragrance to God"? (2 Corinthians 2:15). And it is right to speak of the Church as a lily; for like a lily she shines in the sight of all people, such is the splendour of her deeds. Better still call her lily of the valley, for she is loveliest among the lowly, a lily growing among thorns – that is among those who do not believe and those whose beliefs are tainted. She grows in the thick of the distractions of life that harass the mind and plague the soul. In another way she is like the splendour of the lily among thorns, for God's Church is more dazzling in its beauty than any other assembly.

Reflection

Consider, too, that the lily flower is surrounded by gorgeous petals, and within has a beautiful perfume. So Christ's flesh is surrounded as though by a wall with the glory of the Godhead. Scripture says, "My beloved is white and ruddy" (Song 5:10). White stands for his divinity in all its glory and the red for the beauty of the human complexion which Christ took on himself in the sacrament of the incarnation. The flesh of Christ imparts a sweet odour, for it is sinless. Wicked people, by touching it, blacken their hands with sin. Saints, in venerating it, burn with the sweet incense of their love. Jesus accepts the offering of his loving Church and says to her, "How beautiful you are, my love" (Song 1:15).

Prayer

Lord, how beautiful you are, my beloved, and how delightful (Song 1:16). Not only is there fragrance in an apple, but sweet eating; and your Body and Blood are good food. As an apple tree among the trees of the wood, so is my beloved among the young men (Song 2:3). Your words soothe my innermost heart more than the words of any prophet or apostle. Teach me, O Lord, the way of your statutes: and I will honour it to the end.

16

PASTURES GREEN

Teach me, O Lord, the way of your statutes: and I
will honour it to the end. (Psalm 119:33)

Meditation

Sometimes the Church or the individual Christian rests
along the way in the sweetness of her husband who is
Christ and longs to enjoy him more perfectly. It is like
the Bride of the Song of Songs who runs to the beloved
saying, "Bring me into the cellar of wine, establish love
within me, strengthen me with ointments, restore me
with apples, for I am wounded with love. His left hand is
under my head, his right hand will embrace me. I charge
you daughters of Jerusalem, by the virtues and the
valours of the field not to stir my love nor rouse it, until it
pleases" (Song 2:4–7). She is right to seek him; right to
long passionately for him, for our sovereign has dis-
posed all things admirably for our passage and journey.
First of all he has taken good care to set up for us a
household with a firm foundation of faith. If at any time
he perceives that we are troubled, he waters what is arid
and makes the desert bloom. If we have to go through
patches of bitterness, or temptation, this good general of
ours sweetens what is unpalatable, dispels our worries,
softens what is hard and strengthens what is weak.

Reflection

When an earthly king wishes his army to recuperate, he does not choose to billet them in a wretched little village that is without supplies, or in a desert void of all vegetation. No, he chooses a beautiful city, supplied and well stocked; or if it is a spot in the country it will be a place of pleasant meadows, green pastures and shady woodland. If such kings know how to provide what is pleasant and necessary for their armies, how much more will the good God know how to supply all that is of advantage to those who love him? If they have to march by a way that is unknown to them, he will send scouts ahead to pick out the best pathways for them.

Prayer

Sovereign Lord, earthly rulers consider it beneath them to reconnoitre the way ahead, but when the Hebrews were on the march you "went before them on their way, by day in the form of a pillar of cloud to show them the way, and by night in the form of a pillar of fire. The pillar of cloud never failed to go before them by day" (Exodus 13:21–22). Teach me, O Lord, the way of your statutes: and I will honour it to the end.

17

THE WOUND OF LOVE

Teach me, O Lord, the way of your statutes: and I
will honour it to the end. (Psalm 119:33)

Meditation

Other places of rest to which the Church joyfully finds
its way are the cross of Christ and his tomb. Here the
Church is herself wounded, but with the wounds of
love. Wounds are what Christ received; what he gives
in return is sweet fragrance. From the tree of the Cross
hangs the fruit, fruit that the Church tastes and so cries
out, "His fruit is sweet to my taste" (Song 2:3). To
learn what this fruit is, read on in the Song of Songs,
"An apple tree among the trees of the wood, so is my
beloved" (Song 2:3). We, too, are wounded whenever
we preach Christ crucified, but we are "a sweet incense
to God" (2 Corinthian 2:16). Christ's cross is a scandal
to the Jews, and to the Greeks foolishness, but to us
who believe it is the power and wisdom of God.

Reflection

As often as the Church preaches her Saviour's death,
she is wounded by this wound of love. "Better to be
wounded by one who loves you than kissed by one
who hates you" (Proverbs 27:6). It is well for the

Church to say, "I am wounded with love" (Song 2:5). "Let us expose ourselves to this good wound. Let us expose ourselves to the arrow of the Beloved. For this arrow is Christ who says, "He made me the target for his arrows" (Lamentations 3:12).

Prayer

It is good to be wounded by this arrow, though not all can say that they are wounded with love. The apostles said it; when stoned for his name, they still preached Christ. Paul said it. Though scourged three separate times he continued to prove day and night to the pagan world that Christ should be worshipped. The martyrs say it too, for though they were worthy to be wounded for Christ's sake, they love him still more. Lord, I want to say it as well. Teach me, O Lord, the way of your statutes: and I will honour it to the end.

18

TURN MY HEART
FROM AVARICE

Incline my heart to your commands: and not to
selfish gain. (Psalm 119:36)

Meditation

Saints do not care for money, which they see as so
much loss, provided that they can gain Christ. What we
might look on as profit could cause loss to the soul, for
money can bring the loss of integrity. How I wish that
we might not merely pray as the Psalmist prays, but
that we might also imitate him in the practice of virtue!
What use is it to me to ask God to turn my heart from
selfish gain, that is, from avarice, if night and day I am
calculating how to make more money? Our heart and
mind must assent to any prayer that we pray with our
lips. Jesus can hear the meaning of our minds. He
knows when our hearts are not in accord with our
words. He is not going to answer such a prayer. The
Christian who wishes to pray sincerely says, "Surely I
should pray not only with the spirit, but with the mind
as well? And sing praises not only with the spirit, but
with the mind as well?" (1 Corinthians 14:15). We
must be sincere in wanting to be rid of avarice and God
will be more inclined to hear our prayer.

Reflection

But we are weak. While we want to turn our heart away from money, we are captivated by the sight of wealth, gold and silver, beautiful things, handsome property. We begin to covet the possessions of others. So the Psalmist also says, "Turn away my eyes from looking on vanities: as I walk in your way, give me life" (Psalm 119:37). Those who are going God's way do not notice passing vanities.

Prayer

Lord Christ, you are the perfect way. How can anyone who is joined to you in baptism pay attention to foolish, worldly things? How can they, when you in your own flesh and blood have crucified them all? Incline my heart to your commands and not to selfish gain. Turn away my eyes from looking on vanities, as I walk in your way give me life.

19

INTELLECTUAL VANITY

Turn away my eyes from looking on vanities: as I walk in your way give me life. (Psalm 119:37)

Meditation

We can be vain about many things, not only about our looks, our skills, or our possessions, but also about our intellect. That kind of vanity is one that the eyes of the soul should particularly avoid, because the Apostle condemns it. There are many of whom he says, "Intellectually they are in the dark, and they are estranged from the life of God, without knowledge because they have shut their hearts to it" (Ephesians 4:18). He calls them pagans. Very well, let the pagans be ignorant of something they have never learnt, let them be in the dark regarding what they have never believed, but you have not so learnt Christ. You are not allowed to be ignorant of that which you openly proclaim. Christ did not come in vanity, but in power. He did not come to inflate our vanity, but to illumine our conscience. Christ's work is not to blind the mind, but to enlighten the understanding.

Reflection

Christ has set our hearts on fire so that we might grasp his heavenly commandments and appreciate what we really are. He wants us to understand the grace of eternal life and how we shall enjoy it. We must lift up our minds and make use of our natural intelligence. We are made in the likeness of God. We must seek the things that are above, rather than things that are below, bending our necks to take upon ourselves the weight of this world. We must not pant after silver and gold, for in doing that we shall be held fast by the chains of the world. The poor in this world are strangled by the avarice of the rich, but the wealthy will be suffocated for ever in the next. The minds of the rich are set on vanity; they walk in darkness and they labour in the midst of things that will deliver no profit to them.

Prayer

I know that often the one whose life appears to be overflowing with worldly success is in fact pursuing the path of vanity. Lord, turn away my eyes from looking on vanities: as I walk in your way give me life.

20

A HOLY FEAR

Make good your promise to your servant: the promise that endures for all that fear you. (Psalm 119:38)

Meditation

A holy fear is the right kind of foundation or pedestal for the Word of the Lord. It is the best setting for the Word. The Christian who fears will gain in knowledge, as a statue firmly set on a pedestal gains in beauty. Fear is the ideal beginning, the ideal teacher for the Word. A godfearing Christian who is also well instructed will not totter and fall. Listen to the word of God in the Song of Songs, "His legs are pillars of marble, set in sockets of gold" (5:15). The marble pillars are the apostles of the Church, and they are founded upon the fear of the saints. Peter, James, John, and Barnabas were clearly pillars of the Church, but so is everyone who overcomes the world. The golden foundation on which these pillars rest is well-instructed fear of the Lord, which is the beginning of wisdom. The apostles' teaching rests on that wise fear. It is like a column that stands on a foundation of gold.

Reflection

The fear of the Lord in his righteous ones is a kind of throne for the teaching of Christ; the chair from which the apostles preach the Gospel. The foundation of that throne is the pure gold of wisdom. Or again, as a good statue presents a likeness of truth, so too, do the words of the saints. What a noble foundation is this golden fear which belongs to the people of God! In the prophet Isaiah I read what other virtues he lists before fear, "a spirit of wisdom and insight, a spirit of counsel and power, a spirit of knowledge and piety and of the fear of the Lord" (Isaiah 11:2).

Prayer

Lord, did your servant Isaiah put all those other virtues before fear so that we could be sure what it means to fear you? May your Spirit rest on me, that I may be informed by wisdom; instructed by understanding; directed by counsel; made strong by goodness; ruled by knowledge and adorned by prayerfulness. Make good your promise to your servant: the promise that endures for all that fear you.

21

LEAP FROM HEAVEN

Let your loving mercy come to me, O Lord: and your salvation according to your word. (Psalm 119:41)

Meditation

"See how he comes," says the Bride, "leaping on the mountains, bounding over the hills" (Song 2:8). Of whom does the Church, who is the Bride, speak but the Lord Jesus, the Word, who in his loving mercy comes to save his people? I have always sought for him, and now he comes; I have for ever prayed that he would come to me, and now he does. I want my love to be roused; I think that I have received the wound of love. Now love itself comes running to me. I said, "Come," and he leaped. Over lofty places he bounded so as to reach the Bride. For the bridechamber of the Bride is the cross.

Reflection

He leaped from heaven to the Virgin; from her womb to the manger; from the manger to the Jordan; from Jordan to the cross; from the cross to the tomb and from the tomb to heaven. "He exulted like a giant to run the race. He has his rising on the edge of heaven, the end of his course is its furthest edge, and nothing is hidden from his burning heat" (Psalm 19:6–7). From his Father's heart he leaps and runs forth upon his saints, east and west, from the northern region to the burning south. It is he who rides upon the sunset, and mounts the dawn above the heaven of heavens. It is he who rises above the mountain peaks, and over the hills.

Prayer

"See how he comes!" Holy Spirit, I wish that were true for me. He is Lord of the mountains. He comes leaping upon them. He leapt upon Jeremiah the prophet, and his apostles, Peter, James and John. "As the mountains stand about Jerusalem, so stands the Lord about his people" (Psalm 125:2). I wish I were a mountain that he would leap on me, but as I am not someone of outstanding power and goodness, then let me be a hill, so that the Lord Christ can climb on me. And should he leap over me, may his shadow, as he passes, protect me. Let your loving mercy come to me, O Lord: and your salvation according to your Word.

22

THE SOUL'S RESPONSE

Let your loving mercy come to me, O Lord: and your salvation according to your word. (Psalm 119:41)

Meditation

Just as the church longs for the coming of the Word, so does the devout Christian. "I said I will arise and go the rounds of the city, through the streets and squares, seeking my true love" (Song 3:2). A Christian, too, is a bride of the Word, desiring him, longing for him and praying, praying continually for him. Our prayers must be offered unconditionally and with perfect trust. If our whole being is intent upon the Word, we shall suddenly feel as though we were hearing the voice of one whom we cannot see, and in the most intimate way recognise the perfume of his divinity. This is an experience generally felt by those who have a living faith. The nostrils of the soul are suddenly filled with spiritual delight, and the bride feels the presence of him whom she seeks. She feels his breath and exclaims, "This is he for whom I seek. This is he for whom I long."

Reflection

Sometimes, when puzzling over something in Scripture, when I am at a loss to understand what it is saying, uncertain and perplexed, I rack my brains and suddenly my heart and mind take off. It is like climbing a mountain. The truth becomes clear, like distant hills suddenly coming into view. My mind is enlightened. I can now comprehend that which was previously unintelligible. The Word which had, so to speak, appeared absent is after all present clearly in my heart. Or again when I find things a little obscure, it feels as though the Word has withdrawn from me, and I long for his presence. When he reappears I appreciate that he is in fact there in the search. I know that we are meant to discover him.

Prayer

Lord, I find it hard always to be aware of the presence of your Word but I know that I must continue to look for him, and when I have found him, I must follow where he leads. I must be like the bride of the Song of Songs who sought and found. "My brother," she says, "passed me by; my soul melted when he spoke." Or as the Septuagint translation gives: "Let your loving mercy come to me, O Lord: and your salvation according to your Word" (Song 5:6).

23

MOUNTAINS
AND HILLS

Let your loving mercy come to me, O Lord: and
your salvation according to your word. (Psalm
119:41)

Meditation

The Lord in the language of the Song of Songs "comes
leaping upon the mountain" (Song 2:8). Follow him.
On the mountains and hills are found the Lord's
huntsmen. They track down those who are to be
captured for eternal life. As God said to Jeremiah, "I
will send for many fishermen, says the Lord, and they
shall fish for them. After that I will send for many
hunters, and they shall hunt them out from every
mountain and hill" (Jeremiah 16:16). That is where the
people of God are to be sought, and that is where grace
and good teaching are to be found in the words of Peter
and Paul: not in the valley, where there are tears, but on
the mountain where Christ will enlighten us. When we
read Peter, we hear Christ. When we read Paul, we hear
Christ. Paul healed, but Christ gives light. He who by
Christ's gift was healed, rose up at the name of the Lord
Jesus. Peter raised the dead woman to life, but Christ
gave her light. "Radiant in light are you", says the

Psalmist, "greater in majesty than the eternal hills" (Psalm 76:4).

Reflection

We cannot all be mountains like Peter and Paul, but we can stand on the mountains or on the hills, so that we may be found by the Lord's fishermen and huntsmen when he sends them out. We can be standing in the commandments of the Law and of the Prophets. We can be well and truly versed in knowledge of the covenant between God and Israel as revealed in the pages of the Old Testament, and of the new covenant sealed in the blood of the Lord Jesus.

Prayer

Let those whom you send, Lord, find us ready. Like reapers sent when the harvest is ripe, let them gather us in as though we were good ears of wheat. But what if any are found outside the mountain or hill . . . ? Will it be like those reapers who were sent to separate good wheat from chaff? Let your loving mercy come to me, O Lord: and your salvation according to your Word.

24

CHRIST THE NOBLE STAG

I shall have an answer for those who reproach me:
for I trust in your word. (Psalm 119:42)

Meditation

Let us look at this young stag who comes leaping
towards us. If we do that we need not be frightened of
serpents. The Psalmist was not afraid, for of them he
says, "I shall have an answer for those who reproach
me, for I trust in your word." The stag is that noble
beast that drinks from running waters, with never a fear
for the crookedness of human serpents or for the
venom of their tongues. To him the serpent is not a
threat but an easy prey. Caught among many serpents,
this noble deer feared them not. A gentle young stag, a
gracious gazelle, he is all love. The serpents pretended
to be his friends, but poured out envy. The noble and
innocent stag cropped the pasture among vipers, "but
all the while he prayed for them" (Psalm 109:4 LXX).
They licked their lips with their three-pronged
tongues, but he was nourished all the time on holy
prayer, and even offered it as food to those who
insulted him. "They repay me evil for good and hatred
for my affection" (Psalm 109:4).

Reflection

To those who insulted him he answered a word and the word is food, since "man does not live on bread alone, but on every word of God" (Luke 4:4). He says too, "When they see me, they toss their heads in derision" (Psalm 109:24). They curse but I bless. Those who insulted me, cursed: I, who preached the word of God, blessed."

Prayer

I know how excellent a thing it is to bear insults and not to insult in return. Whoever does not get angry with one who abuses him, will have you as protector. Help me, Lord, to have an answer for those who reproach me: for I trust in your word.

25

CHRIST THE GOOD
SERPENT

I shall have an answer for those who reproach me:
for I trust in your word. (Psalm 119:42)

Meditation

We are not to fear serpents, not even those which are
venomous, and we must remember that as well as evil
serpents there is also the Good Serpent. "Be wise as
serpents" (Matthew 10:16), he instructs us, and of
himself he says, "As Moses lifted up the serpent in the
wilderness, so must the Son of Man be lifted up" (John
3:14). The Good Serpent was prefigured in that serpent
of bronze set up at the Lord's command by Moses. My
serpent was lifted up on wood. He is the good serpent,
a noble serpent from whose mouth poured not poison,
but our remedy. If you know how to adore this serpent
you need never fear other serpents. Those who love
this serpent can say, "There he stands outside our wall,
peeping in at the windows, glancing through the lattice.
My beloved answered, he said to me, 'Rise up my
darling; my fairest come away. For now the winter is
past, the rains are over and gone; the flowers appear in
the countryside'" (Song 2:9–12).

Reflection

Winter being over, the Good Serpent wants to slough the old skin to clothe himself in fresh and golden beauty. He and the stag are the same. The stag wears two horns, the horn of the Law and the horn of Grace. Together they stand for the two Testaments. Swift of foot, untiring in his course, the Stag runs easily through the world in an instant, and his fame extends everywhere. As the good and kindly serpent he does not bite the earlier Law with his teeth. Nor does he wound by his forbearance the later Testament of the Gospel.

Prayer

As the Good Serpent glides into the lap of his beloved, so may he glide easily into the recesses of my mind. May he imbue the fire of love into the very marrow of my bones. May he feed upon my heart that I shall have an answer for those who reproach me: for I trust in your Word.

26

THE CASTLE OF
THE SOUL

Do not take the word of truth utterly out of my
mouth: for in your judgements is my hope.
(Psalm 119:43)

Meditation

"The eye of the Lord," cries David, "is on those that
fear him." Not the "fear" of terror, but a "holy fear".
The Church and the individual Christian have watched
him skipping like a gazelle over the mountains.
Suddenly we see him behind the wall of the house, his
eyes looking through the window, over the lattice. It
makes for joy and happiness, we have our word of
truth, for now we know that the Church and each of
her members are loved by the Spouse–himself wounded
by love. Even when absent he had been present to his
beloved. He was present when she implored him for his
kisses, "Let him kiss me with the kiss of his mouth"
(Song 1:1). He never feels contempt for the prayers and
caresses of his Bride, but loves the breasts of her who
"publishes abroad his wonderful name." In kindness
he leads her into the innermost part of the house and
then, as it were, playing with her love and testing the
strength of her devotion, will often leave her so that she

may seek him. When he returns and is waiting to be invited to kiss her, he will call the Bride to him, so that their loving embrace may be all the sweeter. His words will add fuel to the fire of her love. "Arise," he says, "come, my love, my lovely one, my dove" (Song 2:10).

Reflection

The Bridegroom, you say, would stand behind the wall. He would look through the windows: he would peep over the lattices so as not to be totally absent, nor yet totally present. What is that wall but the one built on the foundation of the apostles and prophets? It is not a wall which partitions one room from another, but one that rests on that sure foundation. The wall behind which the Word will stand. A wall so well built that it will grow up into a temple, preserving, not destroying all that it contains.

Prayer

Father God, may I be such a building, with windows always open to the east. Let your Word come and stand behind the wall, for "the eye of the Lord is on those that fear him, on those that trust in his unfailing love" (Psalm 33:17). Thus the Word of truth will look at me through my windows. In his judgements is my hope.

27

SECRET OF THE LAW

Do not take the word of truth utterly out of my mouth: for in your judgements is my hope. (Psalm 119:43)

Meditation

In the Song of Songs we read, "Arise my love, and come" (Song 2:10). What can this mean? Perhaps, "Rise from the dead," or again "Rise up, free from those chains that surround you. Rise up, because I have risen for you. Unfasten the bonds of injustice, for I have set you free." The Word of truth cries, "Come!" The snares are broken. A Virgin has given birth; her son is born. See the inner wall of division, that which stirred up strife both within and between human beings to destroy their peace, is knocked down. You can come safely now. I long to see your face and hear your voice. Come, no longer to see me as puzzling reflections in a mirror, but face to face. Come take possession of your lover.

Reflection

The Bride, which I take to be the Church, is devoted to her Lord. She sits within the house, protected by the wall of the Law and the Prophets, who in their turn are founded and built of spiritual stones. The walls enclose and fortify a royal palace, not a prison. A palace that is full of joy and delight. Royal treasures are there, which she admires longingly. How might she acquire the wisdom which would describe and explain these riches to her? Though dwelling in the secret place, she needs an interpreter. The Lord Jesus comes to her, "leaping over the mountains." He stood behind the wall of the house – the house of the Old Testament – looking through the window of the Law, and the caverns of the Prophets.

Prayer

The entrances of that house, the Old Testament, are not yet very clear to me, Lord. The keys of knowledge have not yet turned the locks of those doors behind which are enclosed the secret of the Law. But trying to see things as you see them, leads me to hear you calling the Church to rise up through the Law and the Prophets to the lofty heights of the Gospel. The Bridegroom calls the Church dearest, so that she may cling to him and not seek the things of this world. He calls her beautiful, for beautiful are the feet of those who bring good news – and this she must do. He calls her dove, so that she may fly to those things that are above and leave those things that are of the earth. Do not take the word of truth utterly out of my mouth: for in your judgements is my hope.

28

THE OPEN MIND

I shall walk at liberty: because I have sought your
precepts. (Psalm 119:45)

Meditation

Whoever follows the straight and narrow way of the
commandments walks in a broad place. That is why
we read, "When I was hard pressed you set me free"
(Psalm 4:1), and in another Psalm, "In my danger I
called to the Lord: he answered and set me free"
(118:5). The wise person walks in innocence of heart,
and from that fountain of innocence water flows down
spacious streets. The mind of such a one is not
narrowly enclosed within earthly mundane things, but
rather contemplates heavenly things. Those who can
exclaim, "We are oppressed, but are not hemmed in"
(2 Corinthians 4:8), do not suffer from narrowness of
mind. How could they be, whose mouth is always
open so that faith should never be imprisoned?

Reflection

Paul himself explains what it means to enter into a
broad place. He writes to the Christians of Corinth.
"Even if the body is confined, our heart is wide open.
Our heart is not closed, it is you who have closed your

heart against us." None could have felt constrained with Paul, for in him was the depth of wisdom; in him was the breadth of faith. How could anyone have felt hemmed in with one who was the eternally chosen instrument? The constraint was in those Corinthian Christians. Those who are choked inside themselves, who are strangled by the cords of their own wickedness are evil. A miser is a good example. Or someone who every day pushes the boundaries of his own large estates further out, cutting off neighbours from their own lands. Are such people really free, or are they on the contrary narrowly confined for earth itself does not seem large enough for them?

Prayer

Lord, the one who owns an enormous house and a large estate, but still imagines that it is not enough, is confined by the narrowness of the desire for more. The one who is free is very different. If I seek your precepts, I shall walk at liberty.

29

THE CHARM OF MUSIC

Your statutes have become my songs: in the house
of my pilgrimage. (Psalm 119:54)

Meditation

The just console themselves with heavenly judgements,
and are saddened by the sins of others. God's statutes
are their songs. The things that we know very well tend
to be what we sing. It is much easier to remember the
words of a song. We should not lightly skim over what
we read so that we forget what it is we have read almost
as soon as the letters are out of our sight. Even when the
book is no longer in our hands we should be able, if we
have read it properly, to offer ourselves spiritual
nourishment for our souls to browse on from
memory's treasury and from our own heart. We must
be like the animals which the ancient law found clean
and acceptable, those which chew the cud after they
have finished grazing, who give to themselves from
themselves the nourishment that is stored within. Let
the Lord's statutes be our hymn, our song, our psalm.
Let us sing with the spirit, let us sing too with the mind.
In this way we shall never forget his precepts, and it
will not be able to be said of any one of us, "You have
tossed my words behind you" (Psalm 50:17).

Reflection

The true Solomon made for himself singers who would strive with all their spirit to search into divine things so that his church might never want for singers of psalms, nor faint for lack of a song. We learn this from the example of holy David, for while he played and sang, the evil spirit that tormented the heart of King Saul was expelled. The prophets, when about to prophesy, asked that a skilled soloist should sing a psalm. Released by the sweetness of their song, spiritual grace would pour down. In the Gospel we read that music was played in the house of the father who received back the son he had thought was lost. It was played to delight the faithful as they feasted, but he who was without faith was angered to hear it.

Prayer

You yourself, Lord, did not disdain to say, "We sang to you and you did not dance" (Luke 7:32). You sing to us in the Gospel the forgiveness of sins. Let your statutes become my songs in the house of my pilgrimage.

30

THE DARK NIGHT

I think on your name, O Lord, in the night: and I observe your law. (Psalm 119:55)

Meditation

A good Christian should remember the name of the Lord even during the hours of darkness, calling on the name of Jesus night and day. Let not so much as a second pass by that is empty of the holy practice of prayer. Eager students of the physical sciences only sleep when they have to. How much time then should those who are zealous to know God spend in their beds? They certainly should not be bound by the chains of sleep beyond the minimum that nature requires. King David shed tears every night, and rose from his bed to pray to the Lord. Do you consider that you ought to spend the entire night in sleep? When you are alone in your room you should pray all the more to the Lord. It is then you should implore his protection; it is then you should be blameless.

Reflection

Most of all, "when all around is dark and the walls hide me" (Ecclesiaticus 23:18), I must understand that the Lord sees everything that is hidden. It is pointless for me to continue in the words of the son of Sirach, "Nobody can see me, why need I worry?" (*ibid.*) for the "eyes of the Lord are ten thousand times brighter than the sun, observing every step we take, and penetrating every secret" (Ecclesiasticus 23:19).

Prayer

Even if I do not see you, my judge, can I not see myself? Will I ignore the evidence of my conscience? The thick cloak of night does not cover sin, rather it encourages sinfulness. When I have eaten well or drunk deeply, my mind lacks vigour; I grow drowsy. It is then that sexual desire creeps up on me. My judgement becomes obscured, I don't recognise the filth of unchastity; the purity of chaste living is forgotten, and the glory of self-control is not weighed. When Judas went out to betray Jesus it was night. Peter denied him at night. If I think on your name in the night, Lord, I shall observe your law.

31

THE FACE OF GOD

I have sought your face, O Lord, with my whole
heart. (Psalm 119:58 LXX)

Meditation

We read in the Old Testament that Moses prayed to see
God's face, and was told in reply, "No one can see my
face and live" (Exodus 33:20). Let us take this first in a
mystical sense. The law that Moses received was but a
shadow of the law of God. Secretly and mysteriously it
foretells Christ, but it does not reveal him face to face as
does the Gospel. In the Gospel he speaks to us face to
face, and appears as man born of the Virgin. At the
same time he proves by his miracles that he is the Word.
Perhaps it was revealed to Moses, that without faith the
people would die, because, though many saw Christ
face to face, few believed in him. Returning to the
literal sense of the ancient story we recall that holy
Moses asked God to let him see him face to face. Of
course, this holy prophet of the Lord knew that it was
impossible to see the invisible God face to face, but
ardent devotion overstepped the limits, making him
believe that it might be possible. God could himself
become visible to human eyes.

Reflection

Surely such an error is not to be frowned upon? It is a pleasing, though unfulfillable, desire that longs to grasp the Lord with one's hand, and behold him with one's eyes. Moses knew that humanity was made in the image and likeness of God; for when he was chosen by God to set his people free, he was filled with the Holy Spirit. Moses had seen the angel of God, and his glory. Indeed when he saw the bush burning but not being consumed by the fire, he trembled before such light. He marvelled at the glory which he saw, and was drawn to it, both by desire and by grace. He was drawn so that he might more thoroughly examine the burning glory in the bush. He both feared to examine the bush, and at the same time longed to do so. Imagine how he must have longed to see God's face with his eyes?

Prayer

I am sure that Moses, when he thought about it afterwards, found your face to be full of light, full of glory, full of goodness, full of divine power. More than that I can neither say nor feel, for "when we are finished we are only beginning; and when we come to an end we are only starting" (Ecclesiasticus 18:6). I seek your face, Lord, with my whole heart.

32

THE FACE OF
CONSCIENCE

I have sought your favour with my whole heart:
O be gracious to me according to your word.
(Psalm 119:58)

Meditation
Moses was always eager for God. It could be truly said
of him that he sought God's favour with his whole
heart. Or as the sweet singer of Israel says in an earlier
Psalm, "Your face Lord will I seek" (Psalm 27:10). The
good need not fear to see the face of God, for the face of
their conscience will not be displeasing to him. What
must we make then of Moses' praiseworthy desire to
see him? Anyone who hears about particularly noble,
brave or wise people will naturally want to meet them,
imagining them to be almost superhuman. When
powerful rulers, those to whose care and government
part of this world has been entrusted, appear in public,
all rush out to see them. A great crowd struggling to
catch a glimpse of one person. Very often it is true that
the trappings of power lead folk to imagine that they
have seen more than is actually there. Do you wonder
that God's face is so desirable when the whole human
race marvels at one made in his likeness? You will

understand, of course, that those who are charged with some crime will make themselves scarce. Whoever has a good conscience, and is guilty of no crime steps out boldly.

Reflection

I can appreciate a little more from what you say why Moses so much wanted to see the face of God. He was a good man, he was innocent and in conscience was prepared to face God. Moses ardently longed to open up to him his innermost being so that God might know him through and through. With the Psalmist he cries, "Put me to the test, O Lord, and prove me" (Psalm 26:2). Would he want to submit to such an examination if there were anything on his conscience? Would he want to be tested if he knew he was prey to violent passions?

Prayer

Lord, free from sin, Moses eagerly offered himself to you. Yet not even he was perfect to begin with. Before he led the Israelites out of Egypt he met you in the Burning Bush. "Take off your shoes," he was told (Exodus 3:5). That could refer not only to his footwear but also to the way of life that he had brought with him from Egypt. So then in the wilderness you told him, "No-one can see my face and live" (Exodus 33:20). I have sought your favour with my whole heart: O be gracious to me according to your Word.

33

MERCY AND JUSTICE

O be gracious to me according to your word.
(Psalm 119:58)

Meditation

The graciousness of God is revealed in many ways, but chief among them is his mercy. Mercy is surely a part of justice, so that when we give to the poor we are not only being merciful but we are acting justly. "God gives freely to the poor," says the Psalmist, and he goes on, "his righteousness, his justice, stands for ever" (Psalm 112:9). Besides, since the poor are made in the same likeness as ourselves, it would be unjust were they not helped by their fellows. This is especially true since the Lord our God wanted this earth to be held in common by all people, and its fruits to serve the whole world. But avarice controls the distribution of property. If you claim for yourself a right to something which belongs to the human race – or rather to all living creatures – it is only just that you share some part of it, at least, with the poor. Do not deny food to those to whom you owe a share of your good things.

Reflection

To forgive sins, surely belongs to mercy; in fact to both mercy and justice. Scripture ascribes to justice the forgiveness of sins. I read in the book of Wisdom, "A blessing is on the wooden vessel through which right has prevailed: but the wooden idol made by human hands is accursed" (Wisdom 14:8). The "wooden vessel" refers to the Lord's cross, the accursed are those who in their ignorance worship false gods. The justice that belongs to the cross is none other than the Lord Jesus who ascended the wood of the cross and there crucified the debt owed by our sins. He washed away with his blood, the sin of the whole world.

Prayer

You knew that you had moulded humanity from the slime of the earth. You knew that this earth is liable to corruption, and prone to passion. You knew that human beings according to the frailty of their bodies are open to corruption. Therefore being just you forgive me and all frail humankind the sins to which by nature we are prone. Be gracious to me, Lord, according to your word.

34

AT THE CROSSROADS

I have taken stock of my ways: and have turned back my feet to your commands. (Psalm 119:59)

Meditation

If you have set out on a journey and arrive at crossroads or at a place where several roads meet, you will stop and think to yourself which road you should now take. The first, the second, the third or fourth or, perhaps, a fifth road? You would not dream of following a particular road until you had thought about it, and made a conscious decision about the way you should continue. If you are still not quite sure you will stand there wondering which is the road that leads to the city for which you are bound. With all the more reason, we who are journeying to the kingdom of God need to stop and consider carefully which turn to take, because not every road will take us to the heavenly Jerusalem.

Reflection

There are roads that will bring us to a bad end. They have been worn smooth by devilish temptations and they lead to death. We read about such roads in the book of Proverbs, "A road may seem straightforward yet end as the way to death" (Proverbs 14:12). The way that leads to the kingdom of God is the narrower road.

Prayer

The way that leads to you, Lord, is the one I want to find. Help me to look carefully about me, to talk it over in my mind, to consider the matter deeply. Otherwise I might be tempted to take the broad road and thus be captive in the way that leads to hell. Inspire me to think before I act and to weigh up what I am doing. May I take stock of my ways: and turn back my feet to your commands.

35

THE UNTROUBLED
HEART

I am ready to keep your commandments, and am
not troubled. (Psalm 119:60)

Meditation

If desire and greed tempt you, read the Gospel. Let
Christ say to you: "Do not let your heart be troubled."
If terror invades you, read the Gospel. Let Christ say:
"Do not let your heart be troubled, nor let it be afraid"
(John 14:27). Read what the Apostle Paul says: "The
sufferings of this time are not worthy to be compared
with the glory that is to come" (Romans 8:18). If it
feels as though you are sailing upon the sea, huge waves
rising up and a black tempest raging against you, let
Jesus say to you: "It is I, do not be dismayed" (John
6:20). When you enter into any great and serious
conflict, say first: "I am ready to keep your commandments, and am not troubled." With regard to wordly
matters, be prepared to stand not only against things
which you see, but even against those you do not see.
Remember Paul again: "Wars without and terror
within" (2 Corinthians 7:5). You have a war on your
hands. A war against yourself. A war within. It is good
when you are at peace with yourself, enjoying a kind of

serenity. But skilful is the helmsman who can steer a ship in a storm. Therefore when your soul is troubled and your mind in turmoil, keep yourself still under control.

Reflection

Could I appreciate the courage of a steersman who has never been in a hurricane? Should I applaud one who has no idea of what it is like to be in a storm? Of course not! I can, on the contrary, only admire one who struggles against the wind; who goes forward in the face of the billows; who is not afraid when the ship is lifted high by the waves or cast down to the lowest depths. In the same way I must also acclaim the Christian who conquers adversity by patience, and overcomes disaster with courage. One not elated by success, nor broken by misfortune.

Prayer

A war against injustice and sin is being waged within me. Help me to be more fully aware of the powers that are ranged against my soul. Give me grace to think seriously about the battle. Be with me as I make up my mind what to do. Let my battle-cry be: Lord, I am ready to keep your commandments, and am not troubled.

36

THE MIDNIGHT
OF TEMPTATION

At midnight I rise to give you thanks. (Psalm
119:62)

Meditation

Daytime is not enough for prayer. You must also rise
in the night, at midnight. The Lord himself spent whole
nights in prayer, so that by his own example he might
invite you to pray. He was surely asking his Father to
forgive you, but as he was doing that by his own will he
was making it possible for you to be forgiven. The
Psalmist is exhorting you to get up during the night,
especially in the middle of the night in order to pray.
He alerted you in advance that you must rise at night
when he sang, "I think on your name O Lord in the
night" (Psalm 119:55). Anyone can think on, can
remember, the Lord but nonetheless stay in bed.
Anyone can get up in order to pray about things which
make them feel good. But the Psalmist adds. "At
midnight I rise", teaching us to get up in the middle of
the night – and then with good reason goes on, "to give
you thanks."

Reflection

Thanks about what? And why in the middle of the night? I suppose at that hour we are liable to temptation. Is it then we should be giving thanks to God for the forgiveness of our sins? Should we not be weeping for all that offends him; seeking pardon for what we have done wrong; grace to avoid present temptations and wisdom to avoid future ones. At midnight the tempter is assiduous in laying his snares for Christians who drop their guard. Then the spirits of unrighteousness abound. They hasten to persuade us to every injustice and wickedness when there can be no judge to see us, no one present at the crime. No witness of our sins.

Prayer

The tempter sows various arguments in the mind so that one says to oneself, "I am wrapped in darkness, who sees me? Whom do I fear, surrounded as I am and shut in by walls?" (Ecclesiasticus 23:25). The Most High does not see me; my sins do not reach him. He does not bother to regard things so vile. But in reality I know both from personal experience or from what I learn from others, that no one can possibly be free from temptation. Lord, give me strength to rise at midnight to give you thanks for my salvation.

37

HOLY COMMUNION

At midnight I rise to give you thanks: for the righteousness of your judgements. (Psalm 119:62)

Meditation

If midnight is a time of temptation, it is also a time for contrition. The Lord God could have exterminated the firstborn of the Egyptians at any time, but he judged that midnight was the hour which was best for sinners' grief and sorrow. In order to forestall the hour, and to ensure that the angel of death should pass over the Hebrews without hurting them, Moses sacrificed the Passover, the Paschal lamb, beforehand that evening. By celebrating the Lord's Passover, his Pasch as we also call it, and by eating the sacrifice, he knew that the People of God would not be caught by the wiles of the destroyer. The darts thrown at night by the dark enemy would not catch them unarmed or without spiritual food.

Reflection

You are speaking about divine mysteries here. We too, should forestall the tempter's snares by celebrating beforehand the heavenly banquet. We must not allow anything, and certainly not a delicious meal, to keep us from our places at the Sacrament. Without fail we must be present, ready to receive protection. Eating the body of the Lord Jesus brings forgiveness, and is a prayer for reconciliation with God and for his everlasting defence. We ought to welcome the Lord Jesus to ourselves: where his body is, there is Christ. When the enemy sees our guest room filled with the glory of Christ's heavenly presence, he will realise that the place is closed to his temptations on account of Christ. He will take flight; he will retreat and we shall pass through the middle of the night without harm. And should we wake up, the memory of the Sacrament will fill our hearts.

Prayer

After an evening celebration of the Eucharist, Lord, and when eventually I go to bed, I still cannot forget that you have fed me with the banquet of your own body and blood. Should the enemy attack awaken me, grant that I may pick up the weapons of prayer. At midnight may I rise and give you thanks for the righteousness of your judgements.

38

CHRIST THE
MYSTICAL SUN

The earth, O Lord, is full of your loving mercy: O
teach me your statutes. (Psalm 119:64)

Meditation

Jesus has come with forgiveness of sins, filling the earth
with the Lord's mercy. He is sometimes called the son
of righteousness, the sun of justice. The sun in the sky
is commanded to rise upon all. Indeed the sun rises
daily over all the world, but there is also that mystical
sun which has risen over everyone, who has come for
everyone. He has suffered for everyone and has risen
for everyone. He suffered to take away the sins of the
world. Those who refuse to believe in Christ deprive
themselves of the benefit which is intended for all.
They are like those who close the shutters of a room in
order to keep the sunlight out. They do not manage to
prevent the sun from shining over the world, they only
deprive themselves of its light and heat. The sun
remains the sun, whatever they do.

Reflection

Only fools exclude themselves from the gracious light intended for everyone. So too, the rain falls on everyone; and we can thank our merciful God that it gives water to the just and the unjust. Can there be any doubt that the earth is full of the loving kindness of the Lord? The Psalmist sings, "The earth is the Lord's and all that is in it: the compass of the world and those who dwell therein" (Psalm 24:1).

Prayer

Lord, through your Church, your mercy has been proclaimed among all nations; among all nations is found the gift of faith. The earth, O Lord, is full of your loving mercy: O teach me your statutes.

39

THE KEY OF KNOWLEDGE

The earth, O Lord, is full of your loving mercy: O teach me your statutes. (Psalm 119:64)

Meditation

God teaches and enlightens every mind, pouring in the light of knowledge, provided, of course, that we open our heart's door to receive heaven's light. When you are in doubt, enquire diligently, for "the one who seeks, finds; to the one who knocks, the door is opened" (Matthew 7:8). In the words of scripture there is much that is obscure; but if, with the hand of the mind, as it were, you knock on the door of scripture, and if you carefully examine what lies hidden, little by little you will begin to piece together the meaning of the words. It will be no stranger who opens the door to you, but the Word of God. This is he of whom you read in the Revelation of St John, that the lamb opened the sealed book which up to then no one could open. The Lord Jesus alone, by means of his own Gospel, has made plain the enigmas of the prophets and the mysteries of the law. He alone brought the key of knowledge, and gave it to us.

Reflection

The Pharisees thought that they had that key of knowledge. They did not. If they had they themselves would have entered in and learnt the innermost secrets of the sacred text. But, "alas for you scribes and Pharisees; you neither entered in yourselves, nor allowed anyone else to enter" (Luke 11:52). How could they or anyone else have the key of knowledge while at the same time denying the source of all knowledge. So the Psalmist turns to the Lord himself and cries, "Teach me your statutes" for you are the righteous one. Teach me wisdom; for you are Wisdom. Open my heart since you have opened the book which was sealed.

Prayer

The Psalmist's prayer shall be mine as well. Teach me wisdom; for you are Wisdom. Open heaven's door for me, since you yourself are that door. Through you, if anyone enters in, they will possess the eternal kingdom. Through you, if anyone goes in they will never be deceived. Deception will be impossible for they will have entered the home of truth. The earth, O Lord, is full of your loving mercy: O teach me your statutes.

40

THE USES OF
ADVERSITY

Lord, you have done good to your servant: in
accordance with your word. (Psalm 119:65)

Meditation

The wicked of either kind, whether spiritual or human,
are numberless, and they treat the righteous very
badly. For example, should a good person lose a much
loved child, as can happen in this world, or if a fortune
is suddenly dispersed, or any other kind of adversity is
suffered, the unbeliever may say, "Where has your
goodness got you? Just where is the mercy of God
now? Look how you have been punished; look how
much notice was taken of your obedience to God's
laws." Job is an example. He lived an utterly just and
good life. Three men came to visit him. They were
supposed to be his friends, but secretly they seem to
have hated him. When he suffered some terrible
adversities they came to condole with him, but they
actually disparaged him because they were envious of
his integrity. They cast terrible reproaches in his teeth.
They pretended to sympathise with Job, but in doing
so insulted him. A truly good man is not moved by this
kind of behaviour, and neither was Job. Whether he

lost his fortune, and he was a very wealthy man, or his children who were all grown up and married, and his grandchildren, he kept on saying, "The Lord gave, the Lord has taken away. Blessed be the name of the Lord" (Job 1:2).

Reflection

We too, when we are facing adversity, should continue to say, "Lord, you have done good to your servant." The Lord can change what he has done into something better; and can give back that which was lost. If we have lost children, we can become parents of better ones. Is it so difficult for God to give us better gifts? Even if he gives nothing, the righteous person can see that children, who perhaps might have turned against God at a later stage, have been snatched away before they could lose their innocence. To a much greater extent this is true of possessions. It is not difficult to see that a great many people are in danger of losing themselves on account of their riches. There are so many for whom an immense fortune gives rise to sin.

Prayer

Lord, the one who has nothing cannot be blamed for not giving; but the one who has something to give and does not give, is in danger of sin. Lord, you have done good to your servant: in accordance with your Word.

41

GOD'S PRECEPTS
ARE GOLD

The law of your mouth is dearer to me than a
wealth of gold and silver. (Psalm 119:72)

Meditation

Not many people can honestly say that they value
God's law more than all the gold and silver in the
world. Those who can are very rare, especially those
who are prepared to relinquish everything for its sake.
Christ will only find such a person among those
whom he himself has graciously taught. Peter was one.
He could both pray the Psalmist's words and also live
them. He actually said, "I have neither silver nor gold"
(Acts 3:6). He is not using words like a miser, who has
buried his gold in the ground. Nor is he like a rich
person who pores over the daily profit with anxious
care; piling up wealth on wealth; plotting to obtain a
legacy; keeping an unwearied vigil by the sickbed of
some rich invalid.

Reflection

Some commentators on the Psalms take the phrase,
"Law of your mouth" to mean the law of God's word,
understanding it to be the same as the law of God's

right hand. This again accords well with Peter who says to the Lord, "You have the words of eternal life, and should we leave you?" In effect the disciple is saying, "The law of your mouth is dearer to me than a wealth of gold and silver."

Prayer

I cannot desert so great a good to obtain what this world has to offer. The law of your mouth is dearer to me, Lord, than a wealth of gold and silver.

42

YOUR HANDS HAVE
MADE ME

Your hands have made me and fashioned me: O give me understanding that I may learn your commandments. (Psalm 119:73)

Meditation

Even though the substance of our body is mere clay, and we are clothed in flesh, our frame woven of bones and nerves, nonetheless we are without doubt God's most precious work. Consider what goes into the creation of a human being, and you will understand that nothing on earth is of greater value. Human beings are tall of stature, dignified of countenance with beautiful hair. They do not go about on all fours like the other animals, but are upright by nature so that they can freely look up at the heavens. They are not weighed down by servitude; their necks are not encircled with a collar, but they are conscious of their own liberty, eloquent witnesses of their maker. Of course, other animals are beautiful, and are praised for their loveliness, but apart from that there is nothing. Human beings are still more lovely in their souls than in their bodies, combining in themselves the grace of what is eternal with the charm of what is present. Paul writes, "for that which is seen lasts only for a time, and that which is unseen is eternal" (2 Corinthians 4:18).

Reflection

Is that why the author of Proverbs says, "Many a one protests loyalty, but where will you find a person to keep faith?" (Proverbs 20:6). Great is the one who is an interpreter of the work of God, and great is the one who imitates him. It was Paul who said, "Be imitators of me, as I am of Christ" (1 Corinthians 11:1).

Prayer

We cultivate the earth as if we owned it; we use the sea as though it were our own; and we joyfully wonder at the stars of heaven. All of creation would have sunk into oblivion if your providence had not added to your work someone who could enjoy it. Your hands have made me and fashioned me: O give me understanding that I may learn your commandments.

43

JOY IN ADVERSITY

I know that your judgements are right: and that in faithfulness you have afflicted me. (Psalm 119:75)

Meditation

Placed in adversity, enduring painful trials, the Psalmist knew that this was in order that he might be tested. He knew that God's judgements are just, and that he never deserts those who fight bravely. God will never abandon them, and after their sufferings will give them their crown. The Psalmist also knew that the enjoyment of prosperity and success of various sorts generally proves to be a source of temptation. Because of this, greatly to his credit, he humbled himself so that by his self-abasement he might ward off the temptations that come with prosperity, and endure with cheerful equanimity the trials that confronted him. Had he done this only so long as things were going well for him, he would not have been greatly praiseworthy. What is gained by praising God only so long as we are prosperous, or when we are rich, or when there are not trials or vexations to be endured?

Reflection

It is surely magnificent if we praise God's judgements when we are undergoing some trial or smarting from insults. If we do not allow our praises to cease when racked by sickness, or even facing destruction, that too is praiseworthy. It is right that we should always give God glory for his judgements, following the Psalmist who sang, "Let the daughters of Judah be glad because of your judgements" (48:11). These daughters are believers, members of the body of Christ, who seeing the reason for God's judgements always exult.

Prayer

Lord, whoever rejoices, not because things have turned out successfully, but because they are right, has truly discovered eternal joy and happiness. Because of, or in spite of, my faithfulness I was afflicted, but I know that your judgements are right.

44

THE NECESSITY
OF MEDITATION

O let your mercy come to me that I may live: for
your law is my delight. (Psalm 119:77)

Meditation

The one who thinks deeply about God's law will find
that God's mercies are never far away. By those
mercies and that law we have everlasting life. How
could anyone be blessed except by the mercy of God?
Moreover, whoever meditates on the law, is instructed
in the law; and to be instructed by the law is to be
instructed by the Lord, for it is he who utters the law.
Therefore we hear the Psalmist sing, "Lord, happy the
one whom you instruct, whom you teach through your
law" (Psalm 94:12). We too must learn to ponder on
the law. We must not let ourselves be distracted by the
things of this world that fascinate us or held back by
useless vanities. Always, we should remain attentive to
God's law.

Reflection

I recall that Scripture says, "The mouth of the
righteous man utters wisdom: and his tongue speaks
what is right" (Psalm 37:31). That is in the Old

Testament. In the New I read, "The Word is very near you, it is on your lips and in your heart" (Romans 10:8). It is particularly important that leaders in the church should spend time in meditation. Paul when writing to his young disciple Titus says, "Speak what accords with true doctrine, so that what you say gives powerful encouragement in sound doctrine and refutes those who argue against it" (Titus 1:9). To be able to respond like that requires assiduous and painstaking reflection, and not a merely superficial reading of the text.

Prayer

Lord, your servant Paul instructed Timothy to "attend to reading, preaching and teaching" (1 Timothy 4:13). Frequent, regular and careful reading will enable me to share my faith with others. Make your law my delight, that your mercy may come to me and I may live.

45

THE HEART'S FOUNTAIN

O let my heart be sound in your statutes, that I
may never be put to shame. (Psalm 119:80)

Meditation

Great is the heart who receives the Lord. Great is the
heart of one created by him to receive the Word that
comes down from the heavenly virtues and powers.
The Lord himself says, "I will make my home among
them and live with them" (2 Corinthians 6:16). The
Psalmist asks that his heart may be "sound" because the
human heart is stained, so to speak, defiled by
improper thoughts. If thoughts can pollute us, what are
we to say about deeds? Surely they contaminate us
more? We must not allow our thoughts to infect the
secret places of our being. We must be fearful of
polluting with a grievous stain that which we thought
we were keeping pure.

Reflection

Pilate washed his hands, but he could not wash his
heart. He remained blackened by his crime, even
though he washed his hands publicly in a bowl of
water. Even our thoughts can leave a stain. "What goes
into the mouth does not make a person unclean; it is

what comes out which does that. For from the heart come evil intentions, murder, adultery, fornication, theft, perjury, blasphemy. These are the things that make one unclean" (Matthew 15:11, 19–20). If we are unclean within, we must, "clean first the inside" (Matthew 23:26). If we are clean within, we shall be clean on the outside as well. If a stream of water is polluted, it is no use purifying the pool into which it runs. So long as the source is muddy, the pool is muddy. It is useless in the basin if the fault is at the fountainhead.

Prayer

I realise that I must be pure if what I do is to be pure. My heart is the bubbling fountain of my thoughts. From my heart flows either polluted water of impurity, or limpid streams of love. Lord, let my heart be sound in your statutes, that I may never be put to shame.

46

WHEN THE SOUL
MELTS WITH LOVE

My soul faints for your salvation: but my hope is
in your word. (Psalm 119:81 LXX)

Meditation

The Christian who cleaves fast to the Spirit surrenders
all control in order to be united to the Spirit. "Anyone
who is joined to the Lord is one spirit with him"
(1 Corinthians 6:17). The godfearing can long for
nothing except the salvation that comes from God,
namely Jesus Christ. Loving him, longing for him,
Chritians worship him with all their powers and
faculties. They cherish him in their hearts, opening
themselves to him, pouring out their love. Their one
and only fear is that they may lose him. The greater
our desire to cling passionately to our salvation, the
more are we liable to faint. Fainting like this while it
increases our weakness and frailty, at the same time
increases virtue. The Psalmist sings in one place, "My
soul thirsts for you" (63:2), but later adds, "My soul
clings to you, and your right hand upholds me" (63:9).

Reflection

A thirsty person always wants to be at the fountain, and seems not to seek or to touch anything other than it, so that the only nourishment may be love itself. The Lord, holding me by his right hand and giving his own goodness to me makes me something that I was not before. Thus I can say, "I live now, not with my own life, but with the life of Christ who lives in me" (Galatians 2:20). Love was the cause of my fainting. "My soul has a desire and longing to enter the courts of the Lord" (Psalm 84:2). Pouring out my whole self into my love, I melt away; fainting and longing in agonising suspense.

Prayer

Your prophet Jeremiah teaches me that it is possible to faint for your salvation when he says, "Then there seemed to be a fire burning in my heart, imprisoned in my bones; and I have melted away utterly, unable to bear it" (Jeremiah 20:9). Lord, my soul faints for your salvation, but my hope is in your word.

47

MYSTIC SIGHT AND
MORAL VISION

My eyes fail for watching for your promise:
saying, "O when will you comfort me?" (Psalm
119:82)

Meditation

Just as the Christian by clinging to Christ faints so as to
become one spirit with him, so too the eyes of the mind
can fail so as to become one mind with him. For you
must know that the mind's eyes are the eyes of the
inner self, not the eyes which perform the function of
sight. There is a mind, and there are eyes that belong to
the flesh; but those eyes are blind, for they do not see
God. The flesh has grown proud. There is yet another
eye, which is the mind of Christ. By it the Church sees
Christ, who says to his bride, "You have captured my
heart with one of your eyes" (Song 5:9). It is fitting
that Christ is seen by one eye alone, for he is not seen
with the carnal eye. It is fitting, too, that the church,
though she has two eyes, sees Christ more with the eye
of faith. Keen is the eye of mystic sight; mild is the eye
of moral vision. Bright is the eye which sees into the
mysteries of heaven; gentle is the eye that comprehends
the path we should tread.

Reflection

These perhaps are the eyes with which Paul saw truth. He who could not see Christ, or the truth of Christ, before he lost his sight, saw Christ after he became blind. For Paul saw Christ when he said, "Who are you Lord?" (Acts 9:5). With what eyes did he see if it were not with those which he describes thus, "I will pray with the spirit, and with the mind as well" (1 Corinthians 14:15). He also says, so that we may learn what he sees by praying, "Once after I had got back from Jerusalem, when I was praying in the temple, I felt a great fear, and I saw one who said to me, 'Hurry, leave Jerusalem at once. They will not accept the testimony you are giving about me'"(Acts 22:17–18).

Prayer

Lord, give me eyes of faith that do not fail for watching for your promise. O when will you comfort me?

48

ON WINGS OF LOVE

My eyes fail with watching for your promise, saying, "O when will you comfort me?" (Psalm 119:82)

Meditation

When we love someone we wear our eyes out in watching for that person. We long for them to come, and look forward to their arrival. We gaze in the direction from which they will come, content to remain watching for hours. Daily we wait, but still see nothing. In the story of Tobit we read that Anna did this, looking up and down the road, searching for her son's coming; anxiously watching. So did King David. He stationed watchmen on a lookout tower, and when a runner arrived from the battlefield he desired passionately to question him about the safety of his son Absalom. So too, a young and tender wife, standing on a cliff, watches and waits for her husband's return regardless of how weary she is. Every time she sees a ship she thinks that he is on it. She fears that someone else may get to the jetty before her to rob her of the pleasure of being the first to see her beloved. She is afraid she may not be the first to say, "I have seen you again, my husband," as Anna says to her son, "Now I can die, I have seen you again" (Tobit 11:9).

Reflection

Anna cared nothing about dying in the sweetness of seeing the return of the son she longed for. She was like a wife who, longing to see her husband again, leaves her domestic chores and flies to greet him taking shortcuts through footpaths and alleys. And a prophet, shaking off worldly cares, in unsleeping vigil constantly directs the gaze of his inner eyes upon God's word, until his sight fails him. If anyone sees the word of God but as it were from afar, not yet plain and distinct, it is as though he were discerning the ship of the Word approaching his soul.

Prayer

Let me strain my heart to understand the Scriptures. May your word come to me, and understanding be given me. May I see more distinctly and hasten to reach the harbour of truth. My eyes fail with watching for your promise saying, "O when will you comfort me?"

49

WORK AND WISDOM

My eyes fail with watching for your promise saying, "O when will you comfort me?" (Psalm 119:82)

Meditation

Do you consider yourself idle? Of course not. Yet how much of your time do you give to the word of God? The Psalmist yearned for his word, but we so often reveal a complete lack of enthusiasm for it. We put greater value on those who appear to be working with much activity than on those who apply themselves to the study of Scripture or to knowledge about the things of God. Most of us will say, perhaps with a touch of envy, "Look at that man and all he gets through," or "Look at that woman and all the work she does," but we are not inclined to say the same about someone who is studying the word of God. Actually, it is greater work than any other. Think about this. We have to work at being just; temperance does not come easily. Fortitude requires great self-control. These three with wisdom make up the four cardinal virtues, so wisdom itself must only be acquired after much effort. If Christ is just, surely he works in accordance with the word? He worked in the beginning with his Father, for, "through him all things were made" (John 1:3) so that we might understand that he is the creator of all things.

Reflection

Our work is to be like Christ. Those who search for the word are engaged in a great work. At Bethany when Martha hurried about her task of serving, Mary listened to the Lord's word; and she who heard deserved to be ranked higher than her sister who ministered. Martha, I recall, said to the Lord, "Do you not care that my sister has left me to get on with the work by myself? Tell her to lend a hand." But the Lord answered, "Martha, Martha, you are fretting and fussing about so many things; but one thing is necessary. The part that Mary has chosen is best; and it shall not be taken away from her" (Luke 10:40–42).

Prayer

Lord, this reply shows me quite clearly that to know the Word is a greater work even than to care for the needs of others. I wish it were true that my eyes fail with watching for your promise. O when will you comfort me?

50

THE GOOD SOLDIER

All your commandments are true: but they persecute me with lies, O come to my help. (Psalm 119:86)

Meditation

The Psalmist, like a good soldier does not run away. An experienced warrior does not tremble before a battle, no matter how grave the peril. Faithful and ready, the soldier prays for help from God. Soldiers of Christ do not ask that persecutions should cease, but they do ask to be helped in those times. They know that, "Anybody who tries to live a holy life in Christ Jesus is bound to suffer attack" (2 Timothy 3:12). They prefer to suffer persecution, provided that they may live a holy life in Christ.

Reflection

There are many persecutors, not only those we can see, but those we cannot see. Wicked spirits persecute us. Unbelievers as well. All who want to lead a good life are subject to persecution. No period of history is without it. It may even be true that if we do not suffer we are condemned because we are not really wanting to live a holy life in Christ. Battles to keep faith follow close upon devotion. If there are no fights, then it may be that there is no one who wants to do battle for Christ. The Psalmist did not shrink from suffering, but offered himself to the conflict. He knew that he would win glory and salvation, for a person's faith and devotion are strengthened by frequent attack.

Prayer

I know that faith that is not tried and tested soon languishes. He who lies in wait for us is cunning and catches me when I am off my guard. Danger from outside makes us ready for war, and carries us to victory. They persecute me with lies, O come to my help. All your commandments are true.

51

CHRISTIANS NEED
CHALLENGE

They persecute me with lies, O come to my help.
(Psalm 119:86)

Meditation

In times of persecution our faith flourished. The
deepest thoughts of our innermost being, like a beggar
fixing his eyes on a passerby, were intent on God. We
clung to him. Our mind, as it prayed to him, was
without other distractions. Prayer poured out from the
bottom of our heart. Our speech was at one with the
Lord. In our daily meditation we learned to despise
danger. Death itself held no terror for us. Now that we
have finished with this valuable warfare, we who could
not be broken by any battle are being corrupted
by leisure. In time of persecution there were no
obsequious persons to tempt us by subtle flattery.
There was no time to indulge ourselves in the cult of the
body, nor to engage in the sorts of amusements that the
rich and prosperous enjoy. There was no time for
passion. The apostles, when they were beaten or
imprisoned, were glad because by their wounds they
were winning glory. They rejoiced to be considered
worthy to suffer for the sake of Christ.

Reflection

As I understand it they were quite certain about their inheritance, but in this world they cared nothing for titles, office or rank. They did not think of bettering themselves, which tends to excite even upright people. The apostle who received the greatest number of blows regarded that as promotion.

Prayer

Was the Psalmist right, Lord, to look for similar opportunities of winning distinction? He was not afraid of the enemy and he knew that persecution increases our virtue. He did not ask to be persecuted, nor do I, but let his prayer be mine. They persecute me with lies, O come to my help.

52

JESUS OUR LIFE

In your merciful goodness give me life, that I may
keep the commandments of your mouth. (Psalm
119:88)

Meditation

When the Psalmist prays for life, he is not asking for
something which he already possessed, but for something that he wanted very badly – eternal life. He
understood that true happiness is not possible in this
vale of tears, nor in this physical body whose inherent
weakness betrays the reason for our creation. That is
why we need God's mercy, so long as we remain in the
body. We need God to give us life continuously and
without interruption. Only thus can the good person
live daily to God and die daily to sin. If sin could die in
us, we could truly be alive to God, and we would
persevere in keeping the commands of his mouth.
Those who are given life by the Lord truly keep his
commands.

Reflection

The Psalmist first asks the Lord to give him life, and
afterwards promises to keep the commands of his
mouth. It is not our common humanity that keeps

those commands, but human life supported by an eternal gift through the working of spiritual grace. Or we could look at it another way. The Psalmist already knew the old law. In his prayer he asks for the merciful coming of our Lord to give us those decrees by which the old law will be fulfilled. For example, from the old law we know that adultery is forbidden. In the new law we understand that we must even turn away from any desire to commit it. The Father's mouth, who is Jesus our Lord, said that to look on someone and to lust after them is to commit adultery in the heart.

Prayer
In your merciful goodness give me life, that I may keep the commandments of your mouth.

53

YOUR WORD IN
THE HEAVENS

Lord, your word is for ever: it stands firm in the
heavens. (Psalm 119:89)

Meditation

To appreciate the full force of the Psalmist's prophetic
words let us begin by taking the word "heaven" in its
literal sense. By considering that which we can see with
our bodily eyes, we may pass to a better understanding
of what is discernible by our intellects. If the word of
God endures in heaven, then that is what we should
seek to imitate, where the word stands firm and an
impressive array of heavenly statutes endure, and
where in regular succession the Lord's blessings
continue their appointed tasks. Rain, warmth, heat,
these pour abundant fruitfulness over the earth to
nourish it. Thanks to the heavens the year glides
through its days and hours, months and years and its
seasons too: autumn, winter, spring and the sheer
delight of summer.

Reflection

We may look to the heavens for a symbol of our own
lives. Even though we are not producing fruits,

nonetheless we sow in hope. There are seeds from heaven that are sown on earth. And from these seeds we obtain a heavenly vintage. "Sow for yourselves justice, and gather in the fruit of the vintage" (Hosea 10:12*). When what we are working at produces no flower, we must nourish our seeds. We must not allow them to grow wild and wanton.

Prayer

When I indulge in flowery rhetoric, help me to cut back my speech and prune it that I may produce good fruit. If I have too much fruit, cut some away to allow the best to ripen. Lord your word, not mine, is for ever; it stands firm in the heavens.

---

*This translation cannot be drawn from the Septuagint. The NEB translates it thus: "Sow for yourselves in justice and you will reap what loyalty deserves."

54

HEAVEN – THE HEART
OF THE JUST

Lord, your word is for ever: it stands firm in the heavens. (Psalm 119:89)

Meditation

Even in heaven there was the possibility of evil, else how could our enemy have fallen from thence? He must have done something to have been thrust from the heavenly courts. The son of Sirach has no doubts. In Ecclesiasticus we read, "A fool is as changeable as the moon" (Ecclesiasticus 27:11). And experience tells us that heaven sometimes covers itself in darkness. The eternal word stands firm among the heavenly Virtues and Powers, not in the sky. The angelic orders are holy. They are not subject to change. They are not of the earth. But there are heavens on earth, where God is glorified. Listen to St Paul. "As we have worn the likeness of the man made of dust, so we shall wear the likeness of the heavenly man" (1 Corinthians 15:49). These are the heavens who, even while they are on the earth, dare to say, "For us, our homeland is in heaven" (Philippians 3:20). In these heavens are to be found faith, gravity, self-control, learning and a heavenly manner of life.

Reflection

We can be called heaven if we live the lives of angels, in perfect integrity, ruling our bodies chastely and keeping ourselves under careful self-control. Our minds will be still. We shall be gentle and peaceable, merciful and generous, giving to the poor. There is, therefore, a heaven on earth wherein are to be found heavenly virtues. So the words of the prophet, "Heaven is my throne" (Isaiah 66:1) refer more, I suppose, to the hearts of the just than to anything else.

Prayer

Lord, I would consider that person to be heaven to whom Christ comes. He knocks on the door, and if it is opened, he will enter. He does not enter alone, but comes with his Father, for as he himself says, "The Father and I will come and make our home with him" (John 14:23). That word, Lord, is for ever. It stands firm in the heavens.

55

THE LIGHT OF
THE UNIVERSE

Lord, your word is for ever: it stands firm in the heavens. (Psalm 119:89)

Meditation

That person is "heaven" to whom Christ comes. He knocks on the door and enters. See how God the Word rouses one who is idle, and wakens one who sleeps. He who comes knocking at the door always wants to come in. But in us there is something that is not alert; there is something that is not always straightforward. Open the door to him when he comes. Open your mind, open your innermost being. Appreciate the wealth of simplicity, the treasure of peace, the attraction of goodness and grace. Open your heart wide. Run to meet the light of that eternal sun who illuminates the universe.

Reflection

Of course the true light is shining down on everyone, but if we were to close the shutters we should be depriving ourselves of eternal light. In the same way it is possible to shut Christ out by closing the doors of our minds. Even though he could batter his way in, it is not his wish to break in on us in an unmannerly fashion. He never forces himself on those who are unwilling.

Prayer

You are the Virgin's child. You came from her womb, bathing the entire universe in your radiant light. You came to shine on everyone. All who want the glory of perpetual brightness must seize this light, a light which no darkness can take from them. Every day the sun sets, succeeded by dark night, but you, the Sun of righteousness, know no setting. Lord, your word is for ever: it stands firm in the heavens.

56

THE RELUCTANT DOOR

Lord, your word is for ever, it stands firm in the heavens. (Psalm 119:89)

Meditation

Be thankful if Christ knocks at your door. This door is our faith. And our faith – provided that it is strong – makes the whole house secure. Christ comes in by this door. That is why the church says in the Song of Songs, "I hear my beloved knocking on the door" (Song 5:2). Hear him, when he knocks. Listen for him, he is longing to enter. He says, "Open to me, my sister, my dearest, my dove, my perfect one, for my head is drenched with dew, my locks with the moisture of the night" (Song 5:2). When is it that God the Word most often knocks on your door? It is when his head is drenched with the night dew. Being extremely kind he visits his people when they are in sorrow or undergoing many trials, in order that they may not surrender to temptation nor be utterly overcome by grief. The sweat of his brow is the result of the hard work of his body, the church.

Reflection

I must keep awake. If not, the Spouse might come and, finding himself locked out, will go away again. Supposing that I were asleep, my heart not awake, he would go away without even knocking. If my heart is awake he will knock and ask me to open the door. My soul has a door, and to it Christ comes and knocks. He hopes to find his bride waiting up. She must not keep so good a lover waiting or he will quickly go away.

Prayer

I want to open myself to you, for I know you desire to come in. I don't want even to appear to shut you out, or ignore your knocking when my body is sleeping. I do shut you out when I am listless, or careless or very lazy. These are bars that keep you from me. Help me to be chaste, tranquil and watchful for your honour. I know that I do you great wrong if I drive you away when you knock. Lord, your word is for ever; it stands firm in the heavens.

57

WHEN THE DOOR OPENS

Lord, your word is for ever, it stands firm in the heavens. (Psalm 119:89)

Meditation

Sometimes if we delay opening our hearts to the word, Christ puts his hand through the lattice. As the bride says, "My beloved thrust his hand through the lattice; I trembled to the core of my being. Then I rose to open to my beloved. Myrrh ran off my hands, pure myrrh off my fingers" (Song 5:4–5). God first thrusts his hand through the lattice, so to speak, when we begin to recognise him in the work of his creation, which is why Jesus says, "Accept the evidence of my deeds, even if you do not believe me" (John 10:38). From this moment love increases; and once conceived in the depths of the heart it grows there. When Christ's seeds have been poured into the womb of the mind – for it is in our minds that we first receive the word – we desire to drink of him to the full. We rise to let in the Word of God.

Reflection

The Christian soul unfolds herself, laying herself open to the Word. But while she is opening, the Spouse passes on, for often he likes to be sought, more often to be found. If he finds the door closed, he knocks. If the Christian delays a while before opening, he goes away. "My love had turned away and gone by" (Song 5:6). But soon he will return and knock again, hoping that this time he will find the bride ready. The words, "and gone by," could, however, mean that the Spouse had penetrated further, into the innermost being of his bride, just as was prophesied to Mary, "A sword will pierce your own heart – so that the secret thoughts of many may be laid bare" (Luke 2:35).

Prayer

The bride, Lord, in the Song of Songs says that "she is faint with love" (Song 5:8). That is how I want it to be, when I contemplate your goodness. And how I hope it will be when I come to you at the last. Your word is for ever: it stands firm in the heavens.

58

ADVANTAGES OF
SPIRITUAL READING

If your law had not been my delight, I should have
perished in my affliction. (Psalm 119:92)

Meditation

We should take up the practice of daily reading, both
the Scriptures and other books written to help us on
our journey to God. Having read, we should meditate
on it, and after meditating imitate what we have
understood. Let us sweat it out in the gymnasium of
the virtues, so that when temptations thunder around
us they will not catch us off our guard like raw recruits.
Nor let us be like people who have not been given the
right food. Starved of the spiritual nourishment that
reading provides, they have grown miserably thin.

Reflection

No amount of temptation can throw into confusion the
Christian who is well fed on the food of athletes. We
must strengthen the brawn and muscle of our souls
with a banquet drawn from the apostles and their
spiritual maturity. They will make us robust, so that
the juice of the Gospel will be found in us.

Prayer

Lord, may I be constant and painstaking in my meditation so that my memory may have a firm grip on the things of heaven. Help me to be ready with appropriate answers and easily understood examples whenever I am questioned about my faith. If your law has not been my delight, I shall perish in any affliction.

59

I AM YOURS

I am yours, O save me: since I study your precepts. (Psalm 119:94)

Meditation

These words appear to be very straightforward, yet few can in honesty say them. Rare indeed is the person who can say to God, "I am yours". Such a one clings to God with heart and mind and strength, and can think of nothing else. They are like the one who said, "Show us the Father, and it is enough" (John 14:8). No one can say it who is avid for money, rank or power. Many, I dare say most of us, do not find that knowing God is all that we need. Large numbers of people, especially those who are rich, and even whole nations, are convinced that to serve God means having nothing. The Son of God, in whom all things exist, is not enough for them. He who is above all, appears to them as someone poor and needy.

Reflection

The rich man in the Gospel was told, "If you wish to be perfect, go sell all that you have and give the money to the poor" (Matthew 19:21). He did not consider God to be enough for him. He was sad, it is true, for he could not believe that he was being asked to give up less than he would receive. The Christian who says to God, "I am yours," can also say, "We have left everything and followed you" (Matthew 19:27). So said the apostles, but not even all of them. We must remember that Judas Iscariot too was an apostle, and that he sat at Christ's table with the others. He too said, "I am yours," but only with his lips, not with his heart. Satan came and entered into him, and said, "He is not yours, Jesus, he is mine. His thoughts are mine. He turned over in his heart the things that are mine. He feasts with you, but he eats with me. From you he receives bread, but from me money. He drinks with you, but sells your blood to me. Your apostle, but my servant."

Prayer

May it never be true of me as it was of Judas. Keep me studying your precepts. I am yours, Lord. O save me!

60

THE HEART THAT IS BROAD AND THE PATH THAT IS NARROW

Only your commandment has no bounds. (Psalm 119:96)

Meditation

The breadth of the heavenly commandments widens the heart of the Psalmist and of the Apostle Paul. Paul writing to the Church at Corinth says, "We have spoken frankly to you, Corinthians, we have opened wide our heart" (2 Corinthians 6:11). He had done just that so that he might teach them the things of heaven. His heart which had before his conversion been narrow with disbelief and intent on persecution, was now broad with the grace of Christ. And he continues, "Do not close your hearts against us" (2 Corinthians 6:12). If Paul asks this, Christ does so even more, for he it is who has drawn back the bolts. It is as if he is saying, "I do not want my people to close their hearts against me. On the narrow path of virtue, the boundlessness of my commandments must be there to comfort the travellers. I want no one to faint on the way, or find the journey irksome." God's commandment is indeed

without bounds. Why not walk in it? Broad too is the
way of wisdom.

Reflection

We must widen our hearts to receive the full force of
the Apostle's words. "Keep a place for us in your
hearts" (2 Corinthians 7:2). Let us make room for his
words; clothing ourselves in mercy, kindness, humility
and patience. How deep we shall be if we can expand
ourselves to the depth of the heavenly commandments!
The command of charity is all embracing. "Love your
enemies", says Jesus (Matthew 5:44). We shall have
truly included everyone in the warmth of our love if we
do not exclude those who hate us. Paul sets out the
broad commandment! "Bless those who persecute
you: never curse them, bless them" (Romans 12:14).

Prayer

I know, Lord, that it is wrong for Christians not to love
their enemies. When I say Christians, I mean men and
women who are perfect, for we who bear the name of
Christ have taken upon ourselves your divine nature.
Wearing your name, why do I run away from hearing
what that implies? Help me to reveal in my life that
only your commandment has no bounds.

61

OUR HEARTS BURN
WITHIN US

Lord, how I love your law: it is my meditation all
the day long. (Psalm 119:92)

Meditation

In the Lamentation of Jeremiah we read, "He sent
down fire from heaven, it ran through my bones"
(Lamentations 1:13). Love comes from one's inmost
self. It is, as it were, clothed in a texture of heat and
bones. God is kind to send us this fire. He does so that
we may love him and find favour in his sight. As for the
nature of this fire, Jesus himself tells us when he says, "I
have come to bring fire to the earth, and how I wish it
were blazing already" (Luke 12:49)! The fire which the
Saviour of all wishes to see blazing is a good fire. It is
God himself consuming and taking away our sins. Into
the very depth of our heart she pours a burning desire for
knowledge of the things of God. He makes our hearts
burn within us when, reading the holy Scriptures, we
understand, sometimes in a flash of inspiration, a
passage in the prophets which up to that moment had
been obscure to us. Such was the fire with which
Cleopas said his heart had burned within him when the
risen Christ had expounded the Scriptures to him and

his companion on the road to Emmaus. This was the fire of which the Lord speaks to the prophet Ezekiel. "I will gather you together into Jerusalem, as a mass of silver, copper, iron, lead, and tin is gathered into a crucible for the fire to be blown to full heat, set you there and melt you; I will collect you and raise the fire of my anger until you are melted within it" (Ezekiel 22:20–22).

Reflection

I only wish that God's word would come and enter the Church, to be a consuming fire. I wish that he would burn the straw and chaff and rubbish; that he would melt with divine fire the lead of evil that is in most of us. I wish that he would soften with heavenly ardour the iron rigour of our sin. I wish that he would render more beautiful the gold and silver, purifying in the fire of suffering the wisdom of the wise and the speech of the prudent, and thus make them still more precious. The fire of love is indeed very good, refining the heart of every holy man and woman to shine more brilliantly with reverence for the creator.

Prayer

I know one cannot love you superficially. Loving you means among other things loving your law, keeping your commandments and following your precepts with all my heart. High-sounding sermons or pious remarks are of little value. What is required is to walk in the way of your Son, Jesus. If I want to learn how to love you properly, I have only to look at the lives of your saints. Lord, I shall only learn to love your law, if you are in my thoughts all day long.

62

FOLLOWING JESUS

I have not turned aside from your judgements: for you yourself are my teacher. (Psalm 119:102)

Meditation

Not to turn aside from God's judgements involves persevering, steadfastly and firmly on the pathway of innocence. It means we ought not to step from the path, nor turn our backs on the way of discipline and self-control. We must press on, not only in the path of the old law and covenant given on Mount Sinai, but also go forward in the way of the new law, whose splendour is in the gospel. "You who dwell far away, hear what I have done; acknowledge my might you who are near," God says in Isaiah (Isaiah 33:13). The prophet begs the Lord not to be remote from the nations for we "who once were far off have been brought nearer" (Ephesians 2:13). We must understand that we are but human, though made, it is true, in the image and likeness of God.

Reflection

Christ was born of the Virgin for our sake, and became like us. Nations who do not turn aside from God's judgements can say, "You yourself are my teacher."

Through your Son Jesus, you have given us your law. Not as you gave the law through Moses; not as you revealed your judgements through the prophets, but you yourself in your Son through the Gospel.

Prayer

I have not turned aside from your judgements: for you yourself are my teacher. On the contrary, I look to you, Lord, and I know you. Following your paths, I learn the true way.

63

THE HONEY OF
YOUR WORDS

How sweet are your words to my tongue: sweeter
than honey to my mouth. (Psalm 119:104)

Meditation

Hearing the Gospel, so long ago foretold in the
Psalmist's prophetic words, makes it plain how sweet
the words are. They reveal the forgiveness of sin and
everlasting life; they proclaim the resurrection of the
dead, which takes away the sting and bitterness of
perpetual death. How aptly the Psalmist speaks of
these things. Because of them a spiritual grace has been
infused into the very depths of our being. It is because
God's words have become sweet to us, that the Lord
can say to his church, "Your lips distil honey" (Song
4:11). Tell us, royal sage, what this honey means.
Elsewhere it is written, "Kindly words are a honey-'
comb" (Proverbs 16:24). The church eats an excellent
honeycomb. As honey is gathered by bees, so are the
riches gathered by the labours of the prophets. Such is
this honey. It is referred to in the words of the Song of
Songs, "I have eaten my bread and my honey; I have
drunk my wine and my milk" (Song 5:1).

Reflection

I understand therefore that the mystical speech of the heavenly Scriptures is the bread, the solid food, that strengthens the hearts of men and women. Its ethical speech is persuasive. Sweeter and milder it soothes the inner mind and renders palatable to the heart that which the patient finds bitter; I mean penitence for sins. The lips of the preachers distil honey when preaching, provided that their words restore the crushed limbs of a Christian who has lapsed or fallen and now lies in ruins.

Prayer

Words, like wine, have a wonderful power to revive a sinner. How sweet are your words to my tongue: sweeter than honey to my mouth.

64

GOOD PASTURES

Your word is a lantern to my feet: and a light to
my path. (Psalm 119:105)

Meditation

David the shepherd king sang, "He will make me lie
down in green pastures" (Psalm 23:2). What, if not
Christ, are the pastures of the faithful? David was
delighted to find himself there. The holy sacraments
are good pastures, where Christians pick the fresh
flowers that breathe the perfume of resurrection, the
lily which is the splendour of eternity; the red rose
which is the blood that flowed from our Lord's body.
The books of Holy Scripture are also good pastures,
where, in our daily reading, we are fed. By them we are
restored and refreshed when we taste what is written.
Or indeed when we chew over in our minds that which
at first we simply tasted. It is on pastures like these that
the Lord's flock grows fat.

Reflection

There are also good pastures that Christ enjoys, when
he feeds among the lilies in the shining splendour of his
saints. There are further pastures on the mountains
which look down on the valleys. Here Christ feeds

like the roebuck or the fawn. The mountains over the valleys are the lights of this world. Gleaming with unfailing humility they stand out by their goodness. Truly it can be said of them "They do not belong to this world, just as I do not belong to this world" (John 17:14). These, his saints who follow Christ are above the world.

Prayer

This world is the valley and it is full of tears, of mourning and weeping. In your providence you have given us your covenant here so that we may weep and lament our sins. You have given us your word as a lantern to our feet, and a light to our path.

65

CHRIST MY LAMP

Your word is a lamp to my feet: and a light to my path. (Psalm 119:105)

Meditation

Christ really is a lamp to me, when he shines on my face. He shines on the earth. He shines in that earthenware vessel; he is the treasure whom we hold in vessels of clay. Send us oil that we may not fail you; the light of the lamp is the oil. I do not mean earthly oil, but the oil of heavenly mercy and grace; the oil with which the prophets were anointed. Humility is that oil, making supple the stiff muscles of our minds. Mercy is that oil, restoring the broken limbs of sinners who have fallen in rocky places. It heals the sick, for being merciful frees us from sin. This oil which is our good works shines in the darkness, giving light to all. It shines in the great solemnities of the Church.

Reflection

In the parable of the wise and foolish bridesmaids, the girls whose supply of oil did not run out, kept faith and deserved to go into the marriage breakfast. The girls who failed to bring a supply of oil – I mean those who during their life on earth had no faith, no prudence, no mercy – deserved to be shut out on the grounds of infidelity. We must be very careful to keep our lamps burning all the time, and our light shining. For if neither is alight we shall be called stupid and will not enter the bridal chamber of our heavenly Bridegroom. In this body, the light of our lamps is a shining conscience. Conscience is our spiritual eye, which must be pure. If our conscience is pure so will our bodies be. If our consciences remain unenlightened then will our bodies be shrouded in the night of sin.

Prayer

Lord, give me oil in my lamp. When I fast remind me to anoint my forehead. Pour the oil of your spirit over me that my whole being may be full of light. Let the lamp which is your word shine in me, that my eye, the body's lamp, may shine brightly. Your word is a lamp to my feet, a light to my path.

66

LET IN THE LIGHT

Your word is a lantern to my feet: and a light to my path. (Psalm 119:105)

Meditation

Truly Christ is that light. Open your shutters and let in the glorious splendour of his light. Prepare our candlestick. Do not let your body, your garment of flesh and blood, your fragile vessel of clay, obscure the light. We read in St Matthew's Gospel, "When a lamp is lit, it is not put under the meal-tub, (that is the place where the family flour is stored), but on the lampstand, where it gives light to everyone in the house" (Matthew 5:15). Let the light of your innermost being shine through and above the meal-tub of your body. If you cannot be free from them, at least see that your bodily appetites are not overindulged. Let them be content, as it were, with good grain.

Reflection

My conversation, I realise, must never be mere gossip. What I have to say should never be thoughtless or ridiculous. That would be to hide my lamp under the meal-tub. God has power to put my lamp firmly on a lampstand, that it can shine on all who are in the house, and also ensure that those who come in may see the light. The principal lampstand, we have. On him, our leader, we must lay our words; and they will shine on everyone who comes into the Church.

Prayer

There is yet another lampstand, my tongue. Is not my mouth the lampstand? Are not my words the lamp? May they always shine brightly and their light never grow dark. Lord, let your word be a lantern to my feet, and a light to my path.

67

LAMPS OF THE
COVENANT

Your word is a lantern to my feet: and a light to
my path. (Psalm 119:105)

Meditation

Our virtues should shine like lamps. Because there are
many shadows we have need of much light. Great is the
darkness around us, so let the light of our good deeds
shine out. These are the lamps that the law intended to
be kept burning in the tabernacles of the covenant,
not those lamps that the old priests were instructed to
light every day. Lamps such as those burn beneath a
shadow and are daily extinguished. Those who light
them do not see what they are doing, nor do they
understand what they read, taking literally what is
meant to be grasped spiritually. Our body is the
tabernacle, the Ark of the Covenant. Christ came in a
body. "The tent of his priesthood is a greater and more
perfect one" (Hebrews 9:11). That is a greater and
more perfect Tabernacle. Taking with him his own
blood, he has entered into the sanctuary, to purify our
conscience from defilement and dead works. He has
done this so that through our bodies, whose deeds
give witness to the dark and hidden thoughts of our

mind, there may shine instead the radiant lamps of goodness.

Reflection

Those burning lamps of goodness shine day and night in the temple of our God. My body must be kept as God's temple. I must treat my whole body, its limbs and organs as part of Christ's body. Then goodness will shine out and nothing or no one will be able to extinguish it, except me, by my sin.

Prayer

Lord, your word is a lantern to my feet, and a light to my path. Through the light shed by chaste thoughts and loving devotion may your glory shine out in splendour.

68

THE MEASURE OF
HUMILITY

Lord I have been humbled exceedingly. (Psalm
119:107*)

Meditation

Is it not Christ himself whom we hear speaking when
the Psalmist says, "I have been humbled exceedingly"?
In the gospels we read of Christ saying, "Come to me
all of you who labour and are overburdened, and I will
give you rest. Shoulder my yoke and learn from me, for
I am gentle and humble in heart, and you will find rest
for your souls" (Matthew 11:28–29). So let us learn
from him. He says that is what we are to do, and what
he teaches will lead to our salvation. It is significant that
to the word "learn" he adds, "from me". For who can
teach humility if they themselves are puffed up with
pride? Such a one might have plenty of human wisdom,
but with an inflated mind and unruly flesh. Or you
might have someone quite content to be poor, but not at
all pleased to be insulted; or one who can bear the pain
of blows but is exasperated by insulting words, or who

---

*This translation would appear to be peculiar to St Ambrose. The
more usual translation goes, "I have been afflicted beyond measure"
and it reads thus in both the Septuagint and the Vulgate.

has no ambition for high office, but is very hurt or offended by the promotion of someone else.

Reflection

In all these things it is important to preserve the measure of humility. It was pride that first hurled us down. By craving for more, we tend to lose even what we have. Humility is good. It seeks for nothing, but acquires everything that it despises. Did not the Lord humble himself in order to raise us up? He humbled himself even to the cross, but because of this, as Scripture says, "God raised him high and gave him the name which is above all other names, that at the name of Jesus every knee should bow" (Philippians 2:9–10).

Prayer

Lord, I could not dare after seeing all the great things you have done, remain standing before you who so humbled yourself. By your cross you have gathered the church to yourself. Lord, I have been humbled exceedingly.

69

MY SOUL IS IN
YOUR HANDS

I take my life in my hands continually: yet I do
not forget your law. (Psalm 119:109)

Meditation

The Psalmist wants to keep himself safe in God's
hands; for "the heart of the king is in the hand of God"
(Proverbs 21:1), and anyone who can control his own
body and rule his own passions is truly said to be a
king. Is he not governing himself with a kind of kingly
power? Such Christians will not lose themselves, and
no one will ever snatch them from the hand of the
almighty Father or the Son. The hand of God, which
made the heavens firm, obviously does not lose those
whom it holds.

Reflection

Let us consider God's hands. In the Song of Songs we
read, "His left hand is under my head, his right hand
embraces me" (Song 2:6). The bride says this of
Christ; the Christian says it of the Word of God.
Christ is that word. He is also wisdom. We are blessed
for wisdom itself embraces us. The hand of wisdom is
mighty, and his right hand is large enough to embrace

us all. The Church, she who is betrothed to the Word of God, is entirely safe, for "to fear the Lord is the perfection of wisdom" (Ecclesiasticus 1:16). Those who fear God have a whole garrison to strengthen them. Wisdom throws both arms around us and holds us tightly.

Prayer

Lord, you extend both arms, yet each hand has its own special gift. In the right are wisdom and length of days, and in the left are riches and honour. All these gifts are good, but they are different. One good belongs to the here and now, the other good to the hereafter. I take my life into my hands continually, yet I do not forget your law.

70

THE ROBE OF WISDOM

My soul is always in your hands: and I have not forgotten your law. (Psalm 119:109 LXX)

I take my life in my hands continually: yet I do not forget your law. (Psalm 119:109 from Hebrew)

Meditation

The Psalmist has earlier declared that in the presence of the Lord "is the fullness of joy, and from your right hand flow delights for evermore" (Psalm 16:11). These delights are nothing less than eternal life. "Who is this", cries the prophet, "coming from Edom, from Bozrah in robes dyed crimson, so richly clothed?" (Isaiah 63:1). In the Song of Songs we read that the robe the bride wore is eternal life. This is the beautiful mantle which the sentries who guarded the walls wanted to take from her. "The watchmen on the walls took away my cloak" (Song 5:7). Such is the mantle stripped from Adam. The Christian, devoted to God, for a long time has searched for him, and when found holds fast and does not let go of him, until clothed in the precious robe of God's love. Happy are those who are clothed in such a robe. They did not forget the law, but fulfilled it.

Reflection

In shining white splendour the soul ascends from earth, gleaming brightly, wrapped in the robe of wisdom. The angels who keep the gate of heaven ask, "Who is this coming up in dazzling white, leaning on her beloved?" (Song 8:5 LXX). This is she who rested her head, that is all her faculties, on the left hand of wisdom. She opened her hand to the poor, coming to the help of those in need. On them she spent money that she herself had earned, or that had been left to her, not money that was stolen from others. She was ambitious for the glory that is won by good deeds, not for empty honours which the world runs after.

Prayer

Lord, I want to be such a Christian. From the desert of this life I want to ascend in shining white to the garden that is always bright with flowers, bathed in the joy of eternal life, that my soul may be always in your hands.

71

THE OARS OF THE SOUL

The wicked have laid a snare for me: I have not
strayed from your precepts. (Psalm 119:110)

Meditation

Elsewhere the Psalmist exclaims, "O for the wings of a
dove; that I might fly away and find rest." Rest from
the snares laid for the righteous, especially the snare of
avarice. What have you to do with things of the earth,
you who have risen with Christ? "You must look for
the things that are in heaven, where Christ is . . . Let
your thoughts be on heavenly things, not on the things
that are on the earth" (Colossians 3:1–2). Why do you
turn back again to earth? As you consider the things of
God, are you not in Enoch carried away to heaven; in
Elijah lifted up in a chariot, and in Paul raised to
paradise where you spoke of the things of heaven? In
David your prayer was heard and you were given the
wings of a dove to fly away. In Christ you were lifted
up. In the Spirit you were given wings as a bird, for he
descended as a dove to teach you to fly from things of
the earth. The one who asks for the wings of a dove to
fly away and find rest teaches us in a later Psalm that
these wings "are covered with silver and their pinions
like shining gold" (Psalm 68:14).

Reflection

Even if I should sleep my wings will rise up. For there are those who keep watch even while they sleep. The bride of Solomon said, "I sleep, but my heart is awake" (Song 5:2). Even at night the spirit stays awake and keeps watch as the prophet says, "With all my heart I long for you in the night" (Isaiah 26:9). At the words of the Spirit my wings open out and I soar in the golden flight of wisdom. I need fear no snares, for I have wings, spiritual oars, at my service. If my thoughts are sincere and my soul pure then I am a dove. I am one of those to whom it was said, "Be harmless as doves" (Matthew 10:16).

Prayer

The wicked have laid a snare for me, but I have not strayed from your precepts. Lord, help me to understand that if my oars are not very big, I must not be too proud to use little ones. I can be like the sparrow which is very quick to spot the snares. When I have almost, but not quite, been caught by some enticing sin, and have escaped just in time, my prayer shall be, "My soul has escaped like a sparrow from the snare of the hunters; the snare is broken and we have gone free" (Psalm 124:7).

72

CHRIST OUR HELP

Away from me all you that do evil: I will keep the commandments of my God. (Psalm 119:115)

Meditation

Where there is wickedness, it is impossible to keep the commandments. As it stands written in the book of Wisdom, "Wisdom will not enter a shifty soul, nor make her home in a body that is mortgaged to sin" (Wisdom 1:4), and in another place, "The wicked will seek me and not find me" (Proverbs 1:28). But in the Septuagint Christ loves the one who is simple, pure, serene. But between perfect goodness and shameful vice there can be no bond whatever. Christ hates, abhors and loathes what is unclean. "Learn from me," he says, "for I am gentle and humble in heart" (Matthew 11:29).

Reflection

Christ also says, "Come to me, all whose work is hard, whose load is heavy" (Matthew 11:28); but he sends the wicked away. To them he says, "Out of my sight you and your wicked ways" (Matthew 7:23). When he speaks about those whose load is heavy, who are overburdened, he does not, of course, mean burdened with wickedness, but with weakness of the body, or perhaps burdened by the inheritance of somebody else's sin. Can you not hear him say, "I come to the help of those whose work is hard. I have no choice but to hate those who deceive, and those who cheat I have no power to help, for by their lack of integrity they could harm others. Guilt holds them back, grace would free them from the burden of sin. The source of sin is an evil disposition; but a fault is a lapse caused through weakness."

Prayer

Lord, you do not drive the wicked away from you because of your own purity and goodness but because they are doing what is unjust or wrong. It was the Pharisee who said, "I am pure and undefiled," and for that he was condemned. The Psalmist does not say, "I am pure," but, "Create in me a new heart, O God" (Psalm 50:12). Put away from me, Lord, all that do evil and I will keep your commandments.

73

EAT MY BODY

Support me as you have promised, and I shall live. Do not disappoint me of my hope. (Psalm 119:116)

Meditation

Those who trust in Christ are not put to shame. The Christian who hopes readily says, "In you I trust, I shall not be put to shame" (Psalm 25:1). It is wise to say, "I trust", for trust strengthens our hope. It confers a kind of authority on all who hope. You must hope continually, consistently so that no one can ever make you ashamed of your hope. What we hope for is the kingdom of God and the company of the angels. These are spiritual blessings. Hope daily. Hope has no end; it never gives up, not even in adversity. When you are suffering greatly and someone says to you, "What good to you now is your righteous way of life?", keep on hoping; your faith will not fail you. Or if someone should say to you, "What earthly use has all this religion and fasting been to you; or for that matter your love of God or your neighbour? You have been hurt just as badly as those who are wicked or godless," keep on hoping. Do not lose faith; for, even when you are weak, faithful Christ is concerned for you.

Reflection

That I know. He says to his disciples, "Give them something to eat yourselves" (Matthew 14:16). He was worried for fear "they might collapse on the way" (Matthew 15:32). In the Scriptures we have the food of the apostles. If we eat that, we shall not collapse. We must eat it beforehand and then come to the food of Christ; the food of our Lord's body, to the banquet of the Sacrament; to the cup by which the faithful are inebriated.

Prayer

Lord, in the sacrament of your body and blood I am clothed in joy because my sins are forgiven. I can shake off the cares and anxieties of my life and the fear of death. Being drunk with you does not make me stagger, but lifts me up. You do not make me confused in my mind, you consecrate me. Support me as you have promised and I shall live. Do not disappoint me of my hope.

THE PHARISEE AND
THE PUBLICAN

Hold me up and I shall be safe; and I will ever delight in your statutes. (Psalm 119:117)

Meditation

Never forget heaven's kindness, and meditate always on the Lord's vindication of his people. Even when we have done some good deed or other, we should still confess our sin before him. We need his justification. The Pharisees did not accept God's justification, for they refused to repent and be baptised. Anyone who is sorry for their sins accepts his vindication. The one who confesses sin is repentant. As the Psalmist says, "Against you alone have I sinned, and I have done evil in your sight. The sentence that you pass against me is just" (Psalm 51:6). The publican who was in the temple with the Pharisee went out justified because by confessing his own iniquity he was vindicating the righteousness of God. The Pharisee on the other hand was trying to justify himself by asserting his own righteousness.

Reflection

Whoever meditates on the righteousness of the Lord is always humble. It is not a matter of being humbled today but elated tomorrow. The one who ponders the goodness of God is always humble of heart and of a gentle spirit. In this context "always" means not a day and a night, or just a day, it is above time. Even when we are numbered among the angels we shall still be confessing the righteousness and justice of God. When we shall have entered into the eternal glory we shall still ascribe our salvation not to our own merits, but to the mercy of God.

Prayer

I do not want it said of me "What do you have that was not given to you? And if it was given, how can you boast as though it were not?" (1 Corinthians 4:7). Whatever good I have comes from you, O Christ. You are the creator of everyone. Hold me up and I shall be safe; and I will ever delight in your statutes.

75

THE IMPRINT OF
THE NAILS

Pierce my flesh in fear of you: for I am afraid of
your judgements. (Psalm 119:120 LXX)

Meditation

Christians who love the Lord's testimonies, pierce
their own flesh with nails. They know that the old self
is being crucified with Christ, and that on the cross the
weakness of our flesh is being destroyed. Otherwise
the heat of our desires, being unchecked, would grow
lascivious; and the root of avarice in our hearts would
extend its serpentine branches. So pierce with nails, and
destroy whatever nourishes sin. Let sin, with all its
allurement, die in your flesh. Nail to the cross your
desire for pleasure, and give it no liberty to roam. You
must of course use spiritual nails to secure the flesh to
the wood of the cross. Perhaps there is a kind of flesh of
the soul, just as there is a body of the soul. By "flesh of
the soul" I mean carnal thoughts. This is the flesh that
fear of the Lord and of his judgements must pierce,
reducing it to obedience.

Reflection

Should this flesh reject the nails, the fear of the Lord, it will deserve to hear these words, "My spirit must not remain in these people, for they are but flesh" (Genesis 6:3). There are stings of fear that pierce us, and nails of fear that transfix us. To be pricked, is to be spurred on. To be transfixed, is to be put to death so as to die to sin and live to God. The nails are spiritual. The goads are spiritual, for it has been written, "It is hard for you, kicking like this against the goad" (Acts 26:14). Spurred by this incentive, Paul on that road to Damascus picked himself up from the ground, and raised up his heart. From then on his conversation would be in heaven.

Prayer

Your apostle Thomas was transfixed by nails when he said, "Unless I see the holes that the nails made in his hands, and can put my finger into the holes they made . . ." (John 20:25). These were nails of a noble desire. They were the nails, not of perfect faith, but at least of faith that desired to be stronger. Pierce my flesh in fear of you: for I am afraid of your judgements.

76

CHRIST OUR DOCTOR

It is time for the Lord to act. (Psalm 119:126)

Meditation

Yes, it is time to act, O Lord, for your law is being broken. How well the Psalmist puts it, "time for the Lord to act." There is also, "A time to be silent, and a time to speak" (Ecclesiasticus 3:7). The time for speaking has come. The psalm is saying that now is the time for Christ to come, because his law has been broken. The Lord Jesus, who is the perfection, the fullness and the final summing-up of the law, comes. He comes to forgive us all our sins, and to blot out the record of our trespasses. He comes to absolve everyone, and to set sinners free.

Reflection

It is time to act when someone is critically ill, or in great pain. If they are rapidly growing worse you run at once to fetch the doctor, bringing him to the patient as quickly as you can for fear of being too late and the patient getting past help. The more serious the malady, the more urgent is the need for a doctor. This surely is what the Psalmist is doing. He sees the corruption of the people, their luxury and soft living, their insincerity and deceit, their avarice, their drunkenness and he runs to Christ for help. He begs Christ to come, knowing that no one else can help us, distressed as we are by such great sins. In urging Christ to come, the Psalmist will stand for no delay. It is time to act, O Lord. Yes, it is time to ascend the cross for us, and to endure death. The entire world is on the verge of ruin. Come and take away the sin of the world.

Prayer

Lord, bring life to the dying; and resurrection to the buried. Since your precepts cannot save us, help us by your action. In the law is precept, in the Gospel is salvation. It is time for you to act.

77

THE PATHS OF INJUSTICE

I straighten my paths by all your precepts; and I hate all lying ways. (Psalm 119:128)

Meditation

Unless you hate all the paths of injustice and unrighteouness, you cannot be ruled by the precepts of God. Someone might refrain from sins of cruelty, but from early youth walk in the path of fornication, or be led astray by someone who offers love and sex for money. Having entered on such a way of life it seems impossible for them to retrace their steps. Young people especially are prone to such "love". They tend to be incautious, weak-willed and do not take kindly to correction. Someone else might be able to cut down on luxuries of various kinds, but then become greedy for money and avaricious. Such is the way with most sins. Overcome one vice only to find yourself prey to another. It is as though our human nature aids and abets sin. If your life style is frugal and you hate luxury, that very frugality breeds a desire to increase your possessions. And upon the heels of avarice follows robbery. Would it not be better to squander what is your own rather than plunder other people?

Reflection

To continue your theme, some are so afraid of diminishing their hoard of gold that they will not give a penny to the poor. They see mercy only as a loss. Others would never do anything base or dishonourable, but are driven instead by the wind of worldly ambition. They are blown like reeds, this way and that, and cannot stand firm in what is right. Some are content to live as their ancestors, faithfully following their tradition. They refuse to give up the false religion of those ancestors, preferring falsehood to the true faith. Yet other people are so tempted by the circus games and the theatre, and other frivolous amusements, that they do not go to church. Someone else stays away from church, preferring to relax in a beautiful country house. Conflicting interests make them fall into the same error of irreligion.

Prayer

Lord, those who hate the paths of unrighteousness are corrected and put right. Help me to straighten my paths by all your precepts, so that I may hate all lying ways.

78

THE BRIDEGROOM'S KISS

I open my mouth and draw in my breath: for I yearn for your commandments. (Psalm 119:131)

Meditation

We read in the gospel that the Lord Jesus opened his mouth to proclaim the beatitudes. He did this so that he might give his spirit to others. The Psalmist too, opens his mouth to receive the spirit. Jesus says, "Receive the Holy Spirit" (John 20:22). Christ who is all fullness also says to mankind through the Psalms, "Open your mouth wide and I will fill it" (81:10). He who fills all things will fill your mouth. Write what he says in the fullness of your heart, and let your mouth cry out to the Lord. By "mouth", is meant your heart or inner disposition. The soul has a mouth, the soul has members. The Psalmist who is also a prophet *par excellence* opened his mouth to Christ, and was able to speak in parables. He opened his mouth and drew in his breath. He had good reason to say, "How sweet are your words to my tongue, sweeter than honey to my mouth" (Psalm 119:103).

Reflection

The Bride of Christ opened her mouth to the Bridegroom, and his lips tasted sweeter than any honey. So she bore witness and said, "His mouth is sweetness, wholly desirable" (Song 5:16). Being in love with him she held him fast and would not let him go. "I brought him," she says, "into my mother's house, and into the inner room where she conceived me" (Song 3:4). Perhaps, "house" stands for the shining discipline of right thinking and good behaviour, and the "inner room" signifies the deeper mysteries. The bride has reason to yearn for the Lord's commandments, for they are redolent of the honey of divine grace.

Prayer

Is not forgiveness of sin sweeter than any honey? Is not the resurrection of the dead lovelier than any flower? I open my mouth and draw in my breath, for I yearn for your commandments.

79

THE CHURCH'S BEAUTY

Order my steps according to your word: that no
evil may get mastery over me. (Psalm 119:133)

Meditation

In the Song of Songs, the royal bridegroom admiring
the steps of the bride cries, "How beautiful are your
feet in their sandals, O prince's daughter! The curve of
your thighs is like the curve of a necklace, the work of a
master hand" (Song 7:2). The Church is as beautiful as
the bride when Christians hold to the truth, keep the
faith and follow their appointed leaders. Often the
clergy have done wrong; the bishop has changed his
mind, the rich have sided with those who hold power in
this world, but the ordinary Christians have remained
faithful and true. Therefore we can say of the Lord
Jesus, when there is an argument about what is good
and what is bad, in his feet the Word is beautiful. The
next line is also true, "the curve of your thighs is like
the curve of a necklace, the work of a master hand."

Reflection

By "thigh", I suppose, we understand a symbol of
generation. As in "Gird your sword about your thigh,
O mighty one" (Psalm 45:4), which assures us that

when the Son of God had emptied himself he came forth from the Virgin, girded with the divinity of the Word to save the whole human race. The text from the Song of Songs likens the bride to the curves of a necklace which married women often wear round their necks. But these are also the ornaments of a warrior. To compare the Church to these precious jewels, the necklaces of those who have triumphed conveys the idea of her victorious progress. Christ's birth from the Virgin, or if you prefer it, the spread of his body, the Church, throughout the nations means that the necks of all the faithful shine with the beauty of these jewels.

Prayer

Lord, because I am a member of your Body, I too am adorned with the necklace of your goodness, made by the hand of my master. Order my steps according to your word, that no evil may get mastery over me.

80

THE FATHER'S FACE

Make your face shine upon your servant: and
teach me your statutes. (Psalm 119:135)

Meditation

The Lord shines on his saints. He is a light in the heart
of the righteous. When you see the wise, you can
be sure that God's glory has descended on them,
enlightening their minds with the brightness of
knowlege, and with an understanding of the things of
God. God's glory shone even physically in the face of
Moses, transfiguring it and making it glorious. The
Israelites when they saw it, trembled and Moses had to
wear a veil. At the same time as that veil was placed
physically over the face of Moses, another was laid
mystically over the hearts of the Jews, so that they
might not see the true splendour of the law. The face of
Moses is the radiant splendour of the law, but this
splendour does not lie in the letter, but in its spiritual
meaning.

Reflection

As long as Moses lived and addressed the Israelites, he
wore a veil over his face. When he died, Joshua the son
of Nun, whom the Greek bible calls Jesus, speaks with

the elders and the people face to face without any veil; no one was afraid. God told him that he was going to be with him, just as he had been with Moses, and that he would enlighten him, not by giving light to his face, but by the true splendour of brave deeds. In this way the Holy Spirit was signifying that the true Jesus was still to come. For those who turn to the true Jesus and listen to him, the veil will be removed from their hearts and they will meet our Saviour face to face.

Prayer

Make your face shine upon your servant: and teach me your statutes.

81

THE FIRE OF
CHRIST'S WORDS

Your word has been tested in the fire, and your
servant has loved it. (Psalm 119:140)

Meditation

It is quite true that the Lord has sent fire on the earth.
Not to burn it a second time as happened when Sodom
was destroyed by fire; nor to strip our mother earth of
the glorious office which is hers, to bear fruit, to bloom
and to flourish. The Lord is more inclined to build up
and to foster what he has made than to endanger or
despoil it. Why should the innocent environment pay
the penalty of our sin? It is not the fault of nature that
the children she has reared have gone wrong. The fire
that the Lord has set alight is in the New Testament. It
is a fire which sets ablaze our innermost beings with a
passion for the knowledge of God. It feeds the flames
of faith and loving devotion, and makes us long to be
holy and good.

Reflection

Jeremiah was tested by such a flame. He said, "A fire
was burning in my bones" (Jeremiah 20:9). Cleopas
and the other disciple were enflamed by the fire of

those heavenly words as they journeyed with the Lord from Jerusalem to their village of Emmaus. They said, "Did not our hearts burn within us as he explained the Scriptures to us?" (Luke 24:32). This fire of Christ's word is a good fire, for it gives heat but it does not burn – except to burn sins. The foundation of gold, (that is the apostles), was tested in this fire; the pure silver of good deeds is refined in it. In this fire precious ornaments are made to shine more brightly, but worthless stuff is consumed. It is the fire that cleanses the mind and destroys error. That is why the Lord says, "You are clean already by means of the word that I have spoken to you" (John 15:3). This is the fire that burns before the Lord; for unless one carries the burning torch of devotion one cannot enjoy his presence.

Prayer

Light the fire first in my mind, then will the light of Christ shine out for me. Your word has been tested in the fire, and your servant loves it.

82

THE CRY OF
THE HEART

I call with my whole heart: hear me, O Lord.
(Psalm 119:145)

Meditation

If we suffer some physical injury, we generally yell so
that people come to help us. The Psalmist, speaking in
the name of King David, was assaulted, and his
persecutors were upon him. First among these was
King Saul who hated him and harried him with his
army. Later David's own son, Absalom, tried to kill his
father. Not content that his father had fled from his
own flesh and blood into exile, Absalom pursued
David in order to kill him. Even so, King David
suffered less from the enemies that he could see than
from the enemies that he could not see. With the saints,
the contest is not only against flesh and blood, but
against the principalities and powers that rule over this
world; rulers of darkness. These, like robbers, lie in
wait – in the night of this world – to ensnare the human
heart. When David saw the furious onslaughts of those
who were against him, he cried out with all his heart.

Reflection

It is not loudness of voice but magnanimity of heart
that we must employ against the devil. The heart has a
voice, even as blood has a voice, which reaches God.
That is why the Lord said, "The voice of your brother
is crying to me from the ground" (Genesis 4:10). Our
heart cries not with a bodily sound, but with lofty
thought and single-minded goodness. Great is the cry
of faith. That is why, in the spirit of adopted children,
we cry out, "Abba, Father!" (Romans 8:15), and
God's own spirit cries aloud in us. Great is the voice of
righteousness and justice. Great is the voice of chastity.
Through a voice such as this the dead not only speak
but, like Abel, they cry out. The souls of the unjust,
even in this life, do not cry out. They are dead to God.
Nothing in them is holy, nothing magnificent. Their
voices are unlike the voice of those whose sound has
gone out into all the world, and their words to the ends
of the earth.

Prayer

I call with my whole heart: hear me, O Lord.

83

PRAYER AT NIGHT

At midnight I rise to give you thanks. (Psalm 119:62)

Meditation
If someone asks, let him ask continually. If a Christian cannot be praying all the time, let the heart always be ready to pray. The Lord Jesus used to spend whole nights in prayer. This was not because he needed to pray, but because he wanted to give you an example to imitate. For your sake he spent nights in prayer, so that you yourself could learn to pray. From what he has given you, make some return to him.

Reflection
I hear the Psalmist speaking, "At midnight I rise to give you thanks." Should I too rise, then? I doubt if I can keep vigil all through the night. When I pray by night, the splendour of the true sun shines brightly in my heart. Everyone who thinks of Christ, and like Christ, is always in his light.

Prayer

Day follows night, Lord, but on me and all your people, Christ is continually breathing his spirit. In the night when I am wakeful, I will rise and give you thanks.

84

EARLY RISING

Before the morning light I rise and I call; for in your word is my hope. Before the night watch my eyes wake: that I may meditate upon your words. (Psalm 119:147–48)

Meditation

In verse 147 the Psalmist says, "Before the morning light" but in the following verse he is more specific. He refers to another time, "Before the night watch". He is speaking of a definite time of prayer and psalmody to the Lord, just as he does in verse 62, "At midnight I rise to give you thanks." When he speaks of the time before the morning light he means that he anticipates the rising sun. It is a great shame if the rays of sunrise should find one lazing shamelessly in bed, or if its lovely light were to strike upon eyes still closed in heavy sleep.

Reflection

I agree. It would be disgraceful to give an entire night, such a considerable amount of time, to nothing else but rest, nor to set aside any of it for prayer and devotion and spiritual sacrifice. We know that we owe the first fruits of our hearts and voices to God. Every day we gather a harvest for ourselves, every day there is fruit.

Prayer

Lord, inspire me to run to meet the rising sun; and when day dawns may it find me ready. May the dawn's glorious light never rouse eyes that are heavy and drunken with sleep. Before the morning light may I rise and call that I may meditate upon your words.

85

THE PRESENCE
OF GOD

You, Lord, are close at hand: and all your
commandments are true. (Psalm 119:151)

Meditation

The Lord is close to everyone, because he is present
everywhere. We cannot flee from him, if we offend
him. We cannot deceive him, if we sin. We cannot lose
him, if we worship him. God beholds everything, sees
everything, stands by each and every one of us and
says, "I am a God who is near" (Jeremiah 23:23).
Indeed how could God be absent from anywhere,
considering what has been written of God's Spirit?
"The Spirit of the Lord fills the whole world" (Wisdom
1:7). Wherever you have the Lord's Spirit, there you
have the Lord God. The prophet Jeremiah, in the
passage already mentioned, goes on, "Do I not fill
heaven and earth? says the Lord" (Jeremiah 23:24). So
how could he be absent seeing that he fills everything?

Reflection

How could we all have received from his goodness,
unless he were to approach each one of us? The
Psalmist knows that God is everywhere, filling heaven,

earth and sea. He reads in another psalm, "Where shall I go from your spirit: or where shall I flee from your presence? If I ascend into heaven you are there: if I make my bed in the grave you are there also. If I spread out my wings towards the morning: or dwell in the uttermost parts of the sea, even there shall your hand lead me and your right hand shall hold me" (Psalm 139:6–9).

Prayer

You, Lord, are close at hand: and all your commandments are true.

86

YOU ARE NEAR, LORD

You, Lord, are close at hand: and all your commandments are true. (Psalm 119:151)

Meditation

The Lord is near, provided we let in the light. If we were to close the shutters of our house, we cannot then blame the sun for keeping our home dark. It is the same if someone decides to lock up his own mind, fastening the door with the bolts of his own sins, thus stupidly keeping out the splendour of the Word. He is lacking in sense, making himself go blind. Will he have any right to complain that the sun of righteousness refused to come in, or to argue that the light of heaven, is too dim? The Word of God is knocking on your door. He says, "If one of you opens the door, I will come in" (Revelation 3:20). If we don't open the door, it is our fault, not his. Of course nothing can lock God out. Nothing can close itself to eternal light. But he refuses to open the doors of wickedness, and does not wish to penetrate the locked rooms of gross injustice.

Reflection

So God does not detain those who run fom him. He does not force those who are unwilling. At the same time he never wearies of those who come close to him; and his power – the Word that is God – is near to everyone. "All things are held together in him. He is, moreover, the head of the body, the church" (Colossians 1:17–18). In him all fullness dwells. But sin separates most people from him, and of them it is said, "those who forsake you shall perish" (Psalm 73:27). That is why the Psalmist goes on, "my joy lies in being close to God."

Prayer

Lord, I know that you are not far from any one of us. In you we live and move, in you we exist (Acts 17:28). To all of us you supply life-giving grace. To everyone you are present with the gift of your own goodness, especially to the contrite. All your commandments are true, and you are close at hand.

87

CHRIST'S LOVABLE
HUMILITY

Consider my affliction and deliver me: for I do
not forget your law. (Psalm 119:153)

Meditation

In Psalm 22, the Lord, who repeated this hymn on the
cross, says, "I am a worm and no man: the scorn of men
and despised by the people" (v. 6). We may read the
Psalm as though referring to Christ's passion. There he
did not pursue his own interests, but the interests of
others. This is he whom the Apostle Paul means us to
imitate, encouraging us to do so in these words, "In
your minds you must be the same as Christ Jesus: his
state was divine, yet he did not cling to his equality
with God, but emptied himself to assume the condition
of a slave" (Philippians 2:5–7). If we want to imitate
Christ, we must not look for aristocratic birth or for
riches. Though his state was divine, he emptied
himself; and though he was rich he made himself poor.

Reflection

We must not look down on ordinary folk because we
were born into a wealthy or important family. We must
not look down on those who serve us, because we are

powerful. We must not despise the poor, because we have money. We surely are not more important or more powerful than Christ, and certainly not richer than he. For our sake he assumed those things we despise. For our sake he humbled himself even to accepting death, death on a cross, to wipe away our sinful pride.

Prayer

What we lost through the disobedience of Adam, we regained through the obedience of your son, Jesus. Because of this, Father, you raised him high and gave him the name which is above all other names; so that at his name all beings should bend the knee to your glory (cf. Philippians 2:9–11). Deliver me, for I do not forget your law.

88

JESUS OUR
SALVATION

Salvation is far from the wicked: for they do not
seek your statutes. (Psalm 119:155)

Meditation

The peril of the wicked is their own responsibility.
They do not come near the Lord. In fact they put
themselves at a distance. Of their own choice they
separate themselves from the grace of salvation. It is
not salvation which runs away from sinners, but
sinners who run from salvation. Salvation came to the
Jews, and they did not receive it.

Reflection

Jesus is salvation. The coming of Jesus the son of man
was announced publicly. "The son of man," writes
Luke, "has come to seek out and save that which was
lost" (19:10). But the people demanded that a thief be
set free. Jesus they repudiated. Who are they that put
themselves at a distance from the Lord, if not those
who refuse to study his statutes?

But the Christian who really studies them is close to
God, clinging to him. The apostle says to those who
search out God's righteousness and justice. "Now in

Christ Jesus, you that used to be so far apart from us have been brought very close, by the blood of Christ" (Ephesians 2:13).

Prayer

The blood of Christ is our righteousness. Is that why he says to John the Baptist, "Permit us to fulfil all righteousness"? (Matthew 3:15). Lord, salvation is far from the wicked, for they do not seek your statutes.

89

JUDGES AND JUDGEMENT

Numberless, O Lord, are your tender mercies:
according to your judgements give me life. (Psalm
119:156)

Meditation

Personally I think that this verse refers to the quality of
Christ's judgement. The Gospel is not only the truths
of our faith, but also the pattern of morals, and the
mirror of a holy life. I find in the Gospel that the Lord
Jesus took upon himself the mind and tasks of many to
teach us how we ought to conduct ourselves when we
are entrusted with similar tasks. For example, he took
upon himself the role of pastor. He said, "The good
shepherd lays down his life for the sheep" (John 10:11)
and so for the sake of his human flock did not refuse to
undergo a bodily passion. He lifted his weary sheep on
the shoulders of his cross, that he might renew them.
Thus he demonstrates the loving mercy of the true
pastor. He took upon himself the office of advocate;
and we have him as our advocate before the Father. All
through the night he used to pray for us, to teach us by
his own example how we ought to pray for the
forgiveness of our sins. He did not pray all night

because there was no other way in which he could reconcile us to the Father, but to show us what an advocate should be like. A bishop too should be like that, praying assiduously for Christ's flock, not only by day, but also by night.

Reflection

He knew, too, what it felt like to be condemned to death, for he stood before the judge as one condemned. He was Lord of all, yet he did not disdain the one who claimed power over him. He was silent during his interrogation, showing by this that his defence did not lie in loud talk, nor in the pleading and eloquence of the courts, but in integrity and an innocent conscience. When, therefore, he assumed the role of judge he says, "I can do nothing by myself" (John 5:30). Good judges do not act arbitrarily, nor simply follow their own inclinations, but deliver judgements according to law. They know the law, and do not indulge their own whims. They do not arrive at their courts from home with minds made up and everything worked out before they have heard the evidence. As they hear, so do they judge. According to the nature of the case being tried so they try to discern what is right. They follow the law. They do not turn the law upside down. They do not change, but they examine the merits of each case. We then must hear what the heavenly judge says, "I can do nothing, but as I hear, I judge" (John 5:30).

Prayer

Numberless, O Lord, are your tender mercies:
according to your judgements give me life.

90

EASY TIMES AND
HARD TIMES

Many there are that persecute me and trouble me:
but I have not swerved from your commands.
(Psalm 119:157)

Meditation

It is easy enough not to swerve from the Lord's
commands so long as no one persecutes or oppresses
you. After all, who would wish to be so ungrateful as
long as everything turns out well, and everything that is
done is crowned with success? The one who has plenty
of money and who enjoys excellent health will surely
thank God. When the Lord was praising that holy man
Job, Satan said, "But Job is not godfearing for nothing,
is he? Stretch out your hand and lay a finger on his
possessions, and I warrant you, he will curse you to
your face" (Job 1:9–11). Job lost both his wealth and
his children, yet he continued to worship the Lord and
remained in his grace. Therefore Job became all the
more worthy of praise. Do you not agree?

Reflection

I do, but surely there is not merely one persecutor. He
has many servants. We must not let them frighten us,

for "we all have to experience many hardships before we enter the kingdom of God" (Acts 14:21). There are as many opportunities of proving ourselves as there are persecutions. When there are many crowns there are many conflicts. It is in our own interests that there are so many persecutions, because they provide us with better chances of being crowned.

Prayer

I take as an example your martyr Sebastian who was born in Milan. The persecutor had either not arrived or had gone away, or perhaps was somewhat lenient. Realising that there was to be no persecution, Sebastian set out for Rome, because in that city he knew there was zeal for the faith and as a consequence a bitter persecution was raging. There he was martyred, that is to say, received his crown. The city where he arrived as a stranger he has made for ever the place where he gained eternal life. If there had been only one persecutor, Sebastian would never have been crowned. Many there are that persecute me and trouble me; but I have not swerved from your commands.

91

HEAVENLY LITURGY, HEAVENLY LAW, HEAVENLY SANCTUARY

Your law do I love. (Psalm 119:163)

Meditation

No one steers clear of injustice and unrighteousness unless they love righteousness. Thus the Psalmist says, "Your law do I love." In that law you will find justice. You will find it if you welcome the spiritual law and rise with Christ. There you will contemplate the heavenly, the eternal altar, not the altar of the earth which itself has been destroyed and plundered by the enemy. You must gaze upon the Jerusalem which is in heaven, and forget about the city on earth once the home of the Jewish people. On account of the disbelief of its citizens, the earthly Jerusalem was conquered and subjugated by the Roman army. A flaming torch was hurled into it, and it was consumed by fire. Turn your gaze on the prince of priests. Look on him of whom it was written, "Since in Jesus, the son of God, we have the supreme high priest who has come from the highest heaven, we must never let go of our faith" (Hebrews 4:14). He pleads for us every day before the Father.

During his life on earth, his heart was touched with compassion for us. Now he daily brings about the remission of our sins. This is our only hope: the forgiveness of sins for all human beings.

Reflections

Jesus is the sole prince of priests. Before him stand all devout priests who have entered, by the merit of his blood, into the sublime and heavenly sanctuary. This is the law we must love. In this law the true Israelite is set free from all slavery to vice. In this law lies the great sabbath, and the blameless rest of the dead. Here is brought to life the seed of those who have died; given life not through human intercourse, but by brotherly redemption.

Prayer

It is because of your law, that if I want to be holy, I must hate injustice and unrighteousness. I do not mean that I must hate the wicked, for they can often be converted. I must not run from my fellow human beings, but I must loathe and shun sin which can kill. Your law is what I must love.

92

THE DIVINE OFFICE

Seven times a day I praise you: because of your righteous judgements. (Psalm 119:164)

Meditation

It is true that the Psalmist records the actual number of times he devoutly prays, but I think that what he is really saying is that his worship is serene, calm and quite unclouded by sin. I mean that his prayer is offered without anger, without misplaced passion or lustful desires. We, too, when we give praise in the Divine Office with hymns and canticles should try to see that our songs and hymns express what is just and eternally true.

Reflection

I appreciate that the meaning of my prayers should never be uncertain or ambiguous. I must not allow my attention to wander. Nor should any preoccupation over my affairs in this world take my mind away from my spiritual work.

Prayer

Let your righteous judgements always be praised, Lord, by a mind that is tranquil. Let me give you my full attention, rather than just switch off temporarily from whatever else I may be doing.

93

THE TRANQUIL MIND

Great is the peace of those who love your law.
(Psalm 119:165)

Meditation

"Nothing shall make them stumble" (Psalm 119:65). I have said before that perfect loves thrusts out fear; and now I say that it shuts out agitation. Those who love God have within themselves the profound tranquillity of a strong and perfect soul. "No flood," writes the sacred author, "can quench love, no torrents can drown it" (Song 8:7). By "flood" is meant the various passions which are incited by worldly desires and revolts of the body. Yet they cannot overthrow the ramparts of love. One who stands secure in love can say, "Our soul has crossed over the torrent." As the Psalmist puts it, "If the Lord had not been on our side when men rose up against us, then they would have swallowed us alive . . . the waters would have overwhelmed us and the torrent gone over us" (Psalm 124:1–3). Could the water of the sea have extinguished Moses' love? No, for he loved God and trusted that he would let him pass safely through the sea. Those who did not love God were drowned in its waters. By their deaths they paid the penalty for sacrilege.

Reflection

We, too, guided by faithful minds, must cross over if we wish to enjoy the presence of God. If there is not only peace, but much peace in our minds, there will be no attacks, no onslaughts from our desires and passions. Even if there is a battle it will be outside ourselves, not within. We must fight against those who persecute us, even if by silence, victory has often to be conceded to them. Their might is our victory. Consequently they are defeated at the very moment when they imagine they have won. We must not let avarice assault us, nor desire unsettle us, nor depression cast us down, nor lust inflame us, nor pride make us arrogant, nor ambition make us crooked, nor fear throw us into a panic. Peace must abound in us. According to the words of the apostle it surpasses all understanding. Nothing more beautiful can be said of peace. Our goal is the summit of wisdom: it is to have a tranquil mind. We don't want our hearts, in any case so prone to failure, to be disturbed by the tales and fables of the poets.

Prayer

My final goal is righteousness and justice. Unrighteousness must not be allowed to sway my mind. I want to be brave and good, and when my warfare is over to be restored to peace. Great is the peace of those who love your law.

94

PEACE THAT SURPASSES ALL UNDERSTANDING

Great is the peace of those who love your law: and nothing shall make them stumble. (Psalm 119:165)

Meditation

Many things arise to disturb one's peace of mind. It might be that a man's wife, deceived by the crafty serpent, irritates her husband. Or a father might deride his son for the son's faith. Or a husband might wound his wife's self-esteem. In all such trials the righteous person can conquer by recalling the words, "Who will separate us from the love of Christ? Will trouble or worry or persecution?" (Romans 8:35). Virtue is constantly being insulted and goodness is often hated. Take the example of a just person who sells everything and shares the money among the poor, keeping nothing back. As often as not such a Christian is despised, even in the Church, where riches count more than they should. As it is written in the Song of Songs, "If a man were to give up all his possessions for love, he would be utterly despised" (Song 8:7). Do not give up on that account.

Reflection

Such a person does not look for any thanks or payment in this world. The reward is in eternal life. It does not worry a good Christian that people have more respect for wealth than righteousness. In any case if the world were to show great respect for good deeds, and so allow the righteous ro reap a reward for their zeal, could it not then be said of them, "They have their reward"? (Matthew 6:2). Yes, they did their good deeds and got thanked for them here.

Prayer

Ah, but what a wretched little reward compared to the salvation that I might have merited! I must save my wages for the future. I can be quite sure that the more the world insults me, the bigger will be my salary. "What we suffer in this life can never be compared to the glory which is waiting for us" (Romans 8:18). I need not break down under insults; be frightened by danger; shaken by storms; even though death rush toward me. I need fear neither life nor the angels of heaven. I should neither be depressed when things go badly, nor elated when things go well. Whoever has the peace that surpasses all understanding is not to be numbered among the weak. Great is the peace of those who love your law, and nothing shall make them stumble.

95

THE WINGS OF PRAYER

Let me cry to you, O Lord. (Psalm 119:169)

Meditation

A good life makes prayer fly. It provides the spiritual wings that carry the prayers of the saints to God. The spirit by which we pray lifts up the prayers of the righteous and just. All the more so if compassionate and contrite hearts commend them. Earlier in this Psalm the author asked for a lamp for his feet so that he would not go astray in his journey on earth. Now, however, he is almost at the end of his life and is making good progress. The hard part of the journey is over and he straightens up. His prayer he directs to heaven, into the presence of our Lord and Saviour. The Psalmist releases his prayer on the blasts of justice and the gusts of wisdom. It flies on the wings of devotion and faith, for these are the mighty supports of innocence and purity. Sin, being far from God, weighs prayer down. The more weighed down a prayer, the less admirable the life of the one who utters it. The prayer of innocents, however, and the groans of those who are compassionate rise up.

Reflection

Surely prayer does not ascend in a physical way? Even so great a prophet as the Psalmist does not ask that his prayer might approach bodily. To think like that would be to confine God to a physical place, as though he dwelt in some place like the earth, only larger. God, being invisible, beyond description, far from our comprehension, fills all things. And the fullness of that divinity dwells in Christ. When Moses received the law, as I remember, he approached God. The Psalmist, with characteristic humility, asks, not that he himself, but that his prayer might approach the presence of God.

Prayer

It seems to me, Lord, that there is a distinct order to be maintained. The more perfect approach you, but the righteous and just of the next rank are satisfied that their prayers should come to you. Let my cry come to you, O Lord.

96

SILENCE IS GOLDEN

My tongue shall sing of your word: for all your commandments are righteousness. (Psalm 119:172)

Meditation

Anyone who has learnt God's commandments speaks God's word. The one who speaks God's word is not speaking idly. To speak idly is to use the words of mankind. That is why the author declares that from the Lord he has received the grace not to speak with human words. Such speech would be idle, and not only idle but dangerous. For such speech we shall all have to render our account. Yes we have to render an account for every idle word. This is a grave risk we run. There are so many words of God that we might speak, and so many works of God that we might speak about. We have the deed that he did in the words of the Torah, the first five books of the Old Testament and the book of Joshua, the son of Nun. We have them too in the book of Judges, the books of the Kings; the book of Ezra; the gospels and the Acts of the Apostles. All these we leave aside in order to speak and hear wordly things.

Reflection

"Hedge your ears with thorns," says Scripture (Ecclesiasticus 28:24). I wish we could also hedge our tongues. Worse still our tongues are surrounded by thorns that pierce and wound those who speak of worldly things. That is why the enemy frequently pours worldly thoughts into our minds, even while we are at prayer. If we ought not to hear that which does not concern us, still less should we speak of it. As the venerable scripture says to each and every one of us, "Lock away your silver and gold, then make scales and weights for your words, and put a door with bolts across your mouth" (Ecclesiasticus 28:24–25). Let faithful silence lock away our thoughts. May we lock away our words, placing bridles in our mouths, because otherwise we might boast and use unbridled language; or placing weights there so that we can carefully weigh and measure every word that we say.

Prayer

Lord, what are those thorns with which I must hedge my ears if they are not a contrite heart and the fear of judgement? They will pierce, but for my good. They will act as goads, but will not wound me. The wounds given by a friend are for my benefit. My tongue shall sing of your word, for all your commandments are righteousness.

97

THE LOST SHEEP AND THE CARING SHEPHERD

I have gone astray like a sheep that is lost: O seek for your servant. (Psalm 119:176)

Meditation

The Psalmist says, "O seek for your servant for I do not forget your commandments". Lord Jesus, come and seek your servant, come and look for your weary sheep. Come, shepherd, seek your sheep, as did Joseph when he was a lad. Your sheep have gone astray while you are not there, while you delay on the mountains. Leave your ninety-nine sheep and come and look for the one that is lost. Come without dogs; come without wicked labourers; come without hired shepherds who do not know how to enter through the door. Come without helper; come without herald. We have been waiting a long time for you to come. I know that you will come, "for I do not forget your commandments".

Reflection

He comes without rod, but with love and mildness of spirit. He will not hesitate to leave the ninety-nine sheep on the mountains; the ravening wolves cannot raid them there. In paradise the serpent harmed us once, but he lost his bait when Adam was expelled from Eden. He can hurt us no longer. He asks that we come to him, for the dreaded wolves harass us; come to him, we who are cast out of paradise, for the serpent's bite invades us. We strayed from your flocks on the heights where you had placed us.

Prayer

The wolf who prowls by night stole me away from your lambs. Look for me, because I search for you. Seek me, find me, lift me up, carry me. You can find anyone whom you seek. Come then, O Lord, because even though I went astray, "I do not forget your commandments". I still hope for healing. Come, Lord, you alone can recall the wandering sheep, while not alarming those whom you leave, because they too will rejoice at the sinner's return. Come and bring salvation to earth and joy to heaven. Seek no longer through hired hands or servants, but through yourself. Lift up in me that flesh which fell in Adam. Lift me up, not from Sarah, but from Mary. She is not only a pure virgin, but one who through grace is perfectly free from every stain of sin. Carry me on your cross which is the salvation of those who go astray. In it alone is rest for the weary. In it alone shall the dying live.

98

THE SEEKER
IS SOUGHT

O seek your servant for I do not forget your commandments. (Psalm 119:176)

Meditation

Give your servant life, for I have not forgotten your commandments. "I sought him whom my soul loves" (Song 3.1), but I cannot find you unless you wish to be found. You like to be sought for a long time, and you want to be stalked diligently. Your Church, the type of the royal bride, knows this. She knows that you do not want her to sleep as she looks for you, or lie down as she searches for you. You knock at the door to wake her up. You discover whether her heart keeps vigil as the flesh sleeps. She lies down and you wish to raise her up. "Wake up from your sleep," you cry, "rise from the dead" (Ephesians 5:14). You put a hand through the opening to raise her up, but if she is slow to rise you leave her. It is your wish that she should seek you a second time, that she should enquire about you from a great many people. You do not want her to forget to seek you, nor to forget your words. If she holds to your words, you will let her catch a sight of you. You will even let yourself be held.

Reflection

I suppose that once she has deserved to be embraced she will show you her fruits. She will show you that she has not forgotten your commandments, and she will say to you, "Come, my beloved, let us go into the fields. The rarest fruits are at our doors; the new as well as the old, I have stored them for you, my beloved" (Song 7:11–13). By this she means she holds all God's commandments – those of the New Testament and those of the Old. The church alone can say this. To her the Bridegroom replies, "Set me like a seal on your heart, like a seal on your arm" (Song 8:6), for you have kept for me both the new and the old. You are my seal, my image, my very own likeness. Let the image of righteousness and justice, the image of wisdom and the image of power shine in you. And because the image of God is in your heart, let it also be in what you do.

Prayer

Let the portrait, the ikon of the Gospel be in my deeds, so that in all my ways I may keep your commandments. The likeness of the Gospel will shine in me if I offer the other cheek to one who strikes me; if I love my enemy; if I take up my cross and follow you. O seek your sevant for I do not forget your commandments.

99

Spiritual marriage

I have strayed like a lost sheep: come search for your servant, for I have not forgotten your commandments. (Psalm 119:176)

Meditation

In the Song of Songs the royal bride declares, "under his eyes I have found true peace" (Song 8:10). She has searched for her lover who has at last found her and they celebrate their betrothal. In just such a manner Christ, in love with his spouse the church, hurried to the celebration of their spiritual marriage. So too, the church, captivated by the beauty of the Word, hastened to make ready for the wedding. The daughters of Jerusalem tried hard to put it off or to delay it. This made the bride impatient. She said, "I am a wall, and my breasts are towers" (Song 8:8). "My breasts are not small," she says. "How can you say that I have no breasts? My powers of understanding are towers of wisdom. Abundance lies within them, as it is written. 'Peace be within your walls: and prosperity in your palaces'" (Psalm 122:7).

Reflection

Because of her breasts, that is to say, her discernment, the bride considered herself ripe for so great a marriage, but the daughters of Jerusalem still could not believe her. They failed to appreciate how well she understood what was happening. So she tells them, "under his eyes I have found true peace." While they were discussing her powers of understanding she was discovering the peace which surpasses all understanding and keeps our hearts and minds in Christ Jesus.

Prayer

Lover and beloved, Christ and the church have hastened to celebrate their spiritual marriage. As a member of the Church, Lord, I share in that union. The peace of Christ is mine. Come, search for your servant for I have not forgotten your commandments.

100

FINAL WORDS

I have strayed like a lost sheep: come, search, for your servant, for I have not forgotten your commandments. (Psalm 119:176)

Meditation

Delighted with the fruits of the vineyard, the Bride, that is, the Church says, "O you who sit in the gardens, your friends listen for your voice" (Song 8:13). She was delighted that Christ was there and that his friends were sitting in the garden listening to him. They were from the heavenly realms, archangels, dominations, thrones. Mankind was not there, expelled from paradise on account of disobedience to the heavenly commandments. Till now the church had been unable to hear his voice, the voice she so much wanted to hear. Therefore she now prays, "Let me hear your voice" (Song 8:13). "Come, search for your servant." We too, if we wish to sit at peace with ourselves, should be gardens, enclosed and defended. Let us produce the flowers and sweet scent of goodness, and so hear the Lord Jesus speaking with the angels.

Reflection

Surely, because the full-grown Church will be tried by various persecutions, she watches out for the wiles of her persecutors even while delighting in the grace of the Word. Fearing for her spouse, rather than for herself, or rather because it is Christ in us who is the target of the persecutors, she says, "Haste away, my beloved. Be like a gazelle, a young stag on the spicy mountains" (Song 8:14). He hastens away for the sake of the weak, who could not bear too severe temptation. That is why it is written that we should flee from city to city, and that if we are persecuted in one town we should escape to the next. For the sake of the weak then, he must hurry away, or fly to the mountains of myrrh which, in return for martyrdom, offer the perfume of a blessed resurrection.

Prayer

The mountains of myrrh are holy. Your Christ hurries away to them because, "He is founded on the holy mountains" (Psalm 87:1), and they are firm foundations. In us he flees; in the mountains he stands firm, faithful to his post. Paul is a mountain of myrrh, for he can say, "We are Christ's incense" (2 Corinthians 2:15). The Psalmist likewise is a mountain of myrrh and the fragrance of his prayer ascended to you like incense (Psalm 141:2). Come, search for your servant for I have not forgotten your commandments.

APPENDIX:
THE ORIGINS OF
THIS COMMENTARY

The text out of which this manual is composed has been taken and adapted from the writings of St Ambrose (*Expositio Psalmum CXVIII*). They are offered to their fellow Christian pilgrims by two Religious, one whose obedience is to Rome, the other to Canterbury. Both our churches honour St Ambrose, so it is our hope that by following in the path of such a godly Father of the Church we may be led in God's good time to true Christian unity.

Some readers might like to be told a little about the life of St Ambrose. He was one of the towering figures of the fourth century. Governor of Milan and Upper Italy, the drama of his sudden investiture as Bishop of the imperial city was only the prelude to scenes more dramatic still. Confrontation, for the sake of justice, with powerful emperors; persecution for the same reason at the hands of empresses; siege in his own basilica; opposition from within and danger from without; these were all part of the woof and web of the twenty-three years during which he guided the Church at Milan.

His first care, however, was always the instruction of his flock. This he did day after day in his sermons, which are in fact commentaries on Scripture. In these sermons he discerns the lover of God's law, and rebukes the lover of money and the seeker after power. For the sincere he has words of encouragement, for the sycophant he has stinging, and sometimes witty, reproofs.

While realising that few of his hearers can say with sincerity: "I put the Law you have given me before all the gold and silver in the world" (Psalm 118 (119) v. 72), he nevertheless continues to present this ideal before the eyes of his people, knowing that for those who arrive at such a love of God's Law there is "much peace" (v. 165); knowing too that the attainment of such peace is the kernel of the greatest of the Psalms, and the highest achievement of the devout soul.

St Ambrose died some hours before dawn on Easter Day, AD 397. He was not more than fifty-eight years of age.